Jesus on Food

David Muskett

O&U

Onwards & Upwards

Onwards and Upwards Publishers

3 Radfords Turf
Cranbrook
Exeter
EX5 7DX
United Kingdom

www.onwardsandupwards.org

Printed in the UK.

ISBN:	978-1-78815-698-1
Typeface:	Sabon LT
Graphic design:	LM Graphic Design

About the Author

David lives in Surrey where he eats and prepares food as well as being a Methodist Minister in the East Solent and Downs Circuit. Ordained in the Church of England in 1990, David served Anglican churches in Bedfordshire and Surrey. Moving to his present appointment in 2010 he now has pastoral charge of Methodist Churches in Surrey, Hampshire and W. Sussex. He transferred to the Methodist Church in 2013.

To contact the author, please write to:
davidjmuskett@gmail.com

Endorsements

David offers careful interpretation of Jesus in easy-to-follow language. Each of these sermons is a sacramental meal ready for sharing.

Paul Johns
Methodist Preacher and formerly Director of the College of Preachers

David's first book *Jesus on Gardening* was, I admitted, not a title which would have me reaching for a copy from the bookshelf as I am not a keen gardener! However, a book with 'Food' in the title is a very different matter – I wouldn't be able to resist picking it up and, as I did find out with David's previous book, this one does not disappoint either!

"What's it all about then?" – the question I asked myself about David's book as I read it through which, as the reader will find out, is the encouragement David gives us when reflecting on Scripture!

For me the answer came through quickly and clearly as David's book is another great opportunity to immerse myself in the Scriptures, to unpack some of the mystery of my faith in God, and to follow some of the signposts which encourage me to deepen my faith and draw closer to the risen Jesus.

David has a real gift to bring an account of the teaching of Christ to life and the focus of Jesus and food reminded me of the invitation to build my faith around the opportunities for hospitality – offered and received – and allow God to work through all that was offered.

For preachers and congregations this book is a resource providing nourishment which will sustain and strengthen our journey of faith and life.

Rev'd Andrew de Ville
Superintendent Minister, The Methodist Church

As someone who thinks about what they are going to have for dinner while they are eating their breakfast the idea of a book entitled *Jesus on Food* was always going to appeal to me! With chapter headings that make you think, "I wonder what that's all about," and a clear writing style, David doesn't play down the complexity of the subjects he is dealing with but instead presents them in a manner that is easy to read; highlighting elements of Jesus' life and ministry which are often glossed over or perceived as irrelevant to the modern reader. I'd recommend this book to anyone 'hungry' to find the extraordinary in the everyday act of sharing bread.

Laura Evans
Deacon, East Solent & Downs Methodist Circuit

David's second book is as warmly and seductively written as his first. He draws his readers with humour and the skills of a consummate preacher into the first century world of Jesus, before challenging us with profound theological truths and practical advice for our lives in the twenty-first century. Each chapter could be described as well-kneaded dough that gradually rises to feed us with perfectly baked food from the Master's table! I would endorse this book for four important reasons:

1. It is firmly grounded in God's Word, the Bible, as any sermon should be.
2. It constantly points us to Jesus, 'the pioneer and perfecter of our faith'.
3. It excites me with the constant revelations from the biblical text to want to keep reading more!
4. It gives us the space to reflect on what is said and draw some of our own conclusions

I'm sure readers will look at both the teaching of Jesus and their own relationship with food in a new light after reading this book!

Keith Field
Elder, Cranleigh Baptist Church

To Marian,
my companion –
the one who eats bread with me

Contents

Jesus on Food

Foreword by Andrew Wood

Food is essential to human life; most experts reckon that we can survive only a few days in good health without it. But there is also the spiritual element of food – eating together, really living as opposed to just existing, expressing hospitality and care for others in need. We might add that Jesus uses meals and talks about food to explore and explain the Kingdom of God.

In this book, David Muskett guides us around the spirituality of food in the Gospels. It has been said that a text without a context is a pretext! David is certainly very attentive to the context – biblical, sociological, geographical, narrative – out of which his sermons spring. He is very concerned to lay out the meaning of a text as well as its content – to ask the question, "So, what's that all about?" David covers a wide range of texts, some very familiar to which he brings new insights, and some you have probably never thought of preaching or discussing. Some highlights are Peter and Matthew's journeys into discipleship via a fishing expedition and a party, Jesus on fasting and hospitality – and four final meals in holy week and beyond which really help our understanding of Easter. There's even one on food that others know nothing about.

So, as you read these sermons, you'll be invited into the world of the Gospels; to live with people in their homes, marketplaces and at their tables. You'll enter the stories in ways that are accessible – and do wait for those important and challenging questions at the end.

A good resource if you're a preacher or small group leader – or just interested in a second look at what Jesus says.

Rev'd Dr Andrew Wood
Chair, Southampton Methodist District

Jesus on Food

Introduction

Jesus on Food seemed to be the obvious sequel to *Jesus on Gardening*. As with the previous title, this book contains some sermons adapted after being preached and others which have been written for the book. All of them have, I hope, a sense of preaching for a congregation in mind rather than simply a written exercise.

Many thanks to Laura Evans and Maria Howard who, on a Southampton Methodist District Ministers' Conference after some discussion about the possibilities for a follow-up to *Jesus on Gardening,* went away and, instead of sleeping, came up with eighteen chapter suggestions. I haven't used all of them and I have added some others, but their suggestions were an invaluable starter.

Many thanks also to Marian, who eats with me and talks with me and encourages me as well as gardens with me. Thank you to Marian and to Zoë for reading my draft, correcting grammar and punctuation, and pointing out when sentences needed to be shorter!

Rather than 'Sermon Notes for Preachers and Listeners' as there were in *Jesus on Gardening*, there are two preaching tools which run through the book. The first is the question, "What's that all about, then?" I use this to draw a distinction with "What happened?" "What happened?" gets us a certain distance with a text; it helps us with the essential knowledge of the contents of a text. But asking, "What's that all about, then?" helps us realise that there's more to it than knowing the content. What's in the text, whether it's story or teaching or narrative, is there for a reason. We have it in the Bible because it meant something to the original writer and it can mean something to the modern reader.

That brings us to the other preaching tool that is evidently used in every chapter (and referred to in most). It's what I describe as the "first tool of biblical interpretation". That tool is context. As a tool it's more of a socket set than a spanner as there are so many aspects to the context of any particular text.

Different aspects of context may be more enlightening than others for different passages. It may be context in the sense of where the passage comes in the Bible; it may be what sort of passage it is (story, narrative, teaching, controversy, conversation...) In other parts of the Bible it might be one of several different sorts of literature.

Then there are other kinds of context that help with interpretation: geographical, sociological, political, cultural... All of these (and possibly others) are employed at some point to aid our interpretation of what Jesus said and did. They help to bridge the gap between Jesus' world of first century Palestine and the twenty-first century world of a congregation in Britain (in my case).

That brings me to the other context that has a bearing on the interpretation of a text: the context in which it is read and spoken (or written) about. The preacher needs to have in mind who is in the congregation, where the congregation is, what they're interested in, how old they might be, what their outlook on the world might be, how much they might know both about the world of the Bible and about their own world.

Obviously, no congregation will be completely homogenous, so we have to allow for diversity. You can't please all of the people all of the time, but it's a recipe for a shrinking congregation if you please some of the people all of the time and some of the people none of the time.

Most discussions of preaching include something about length. Some congregations start fidgeting if a sermon is more than ten minutes; others feel cheated if it is less than twenty-five. The sermons in this book would mostly take about fifteen minutes to preach as they are. They are therefore slightly shorter than many I preach now in a Methodist setting and slightly longer than at a typical Anglican 8am communion service. That shouldn't make a difference to their use. Preachers will be used to the 'adopt and adapt' principle with sermon ideas. I hope that those who more often listen rather than speak during the sermon will find that these give food for thought and supplement their weekly diet. (Pun absolutely intended.)

David Muskett
Haslemere

1

Jesus on Mass Catering

The Feeding of the Four/Five Thousand

Matthew 14:13-21

When Jesus heard what had happened, he withdrew by boat privately to a solitary place. Hearing of this, the crowds followed him on foot from the towns. When Jesus landed and saw a large crowd, he had compassion on them and healed those who were ill.

As evening approached, the disciples came to him and said, 'This is a remote place, and it's already getting late. Send the crowds away, so that they can go to the villages and buy themselves some food.'

Jesus replied, 'They do not need to go away. You give them something to eat.'

'We have here only five loaves of bread and two fish,' they answered.

'Bring them here to me,' he said. And he told the people to sit down on the grass. Taking the five loaves and the two fish and looking up to heaven, he gave thanks and broke the loaves. Then he gave them to the disciples, and the disciples

gave them to the people. They all ate and were satisfied, and the disciples picked up twelve basketfuls of broken pieces that were left over. The number of those who ate was about five thousand men, besides women and children.

A principle of most chapters in this book and of my preaching and teaching from the Bible is that when we read any passage in the Bible, we're not just reading to find out what is described – we don't just want to know what happened. We also ask ourselves another question. Most of the congregations where I preach regularly can now tell me what that question is:

"What's that all about, then?"[1]

We don't just want to know what happened, we want to know what it's about. What's the significance of the story? What is the writer trying to tell us in addition to the events described?

We read and talk about the passage in order to interpret the events and the account we have of them. This leads us to another question:

"What's the first tool in our toolbox of biblical interpretation?"[2]

Answer: "Context."

So, to start at the beginning of Matthew's account of the incident we know as the 'Feeding of the Five Thousand', we realise it's not just an account of Jesus feeding five thousand people. As a matter of detail, a quick glance at the end of the passage shows us that he fed five thousand men and there were women and children present as well. So the total may be more like ten thousand people.

But there are two other statements in the first two verses of this passage that are not to do with the feeding but give us some other information:

"When Jesus heard what had happened…" prompts us to look at the verses immediately before which give an account of the beheading of John the Baptist.

On hearing this news Jesus took the decision to go to a lonely place by himself. This may simply have been for the obvious human

---

[1] Having an opportunity to join in early in the sermon assists engagement on the part of members of the congregation.

[2] It has not been scientifically researched but about 90% of interpretation is to be found in an examination of context: biblical, literary, historical, geographical, political, social…

need to grieve for the death of a relative. It may also relate to Jesus' consciousness of his vocation. He had withdrawn to the wilderness – a lonely place – before he began his ministry. Now he does the same as the focus shifts from John to him. The preparation must be complete because John is now off the scene. From here on it's all down to him.

A further look at the lead-up to the feeding story tells us that there is a large crowd around.

It is not such a lonely place after all.

Jesus' reaction to the presence of the crowd is not only interesting in terms of building the picture of the event; it also tells us something of what it might be all about. Jesus is filled with pity and he heals the sick amongst them. Mark's account of the same event puts the phrase in here that they were *"...like sheep without a shepherd. So he began teaching them many things."*

A summary might be that he both taught and demonstrated the way God's Kingdom works.

Then it transpires that this crowd is hungry. They've come a long way, they're in what was supposed to be a lonely place and they've nothing to eat.

So, first, what happens?[3]

- Jesus announces to the disciples that the crowd are to be fed.
- The disciples raise practical difficulties about the supply of bread in the area.
- Jesus then feeds the crowd using the meagre resources of five loaves and two fish, that is all that can be found.

It is a familiar story; it's in all four Gospels and there's another that is very similar but with different numbers just a chapter later and also in Mark.[4]

We might therefore ask the question, "What's that all about?" Why tell both? The clue is in the numbers. The number twelve is always significant. There were twelve baskets of leftover pieces; there were twelve disciples; and there were also twelve tribes of Israel.

---

[3] At this point we're putting the story together. Asking the question enables a congregation to participate by telling a well-known story which they have also just heard read.

[4] Matthew 15:29-39; Mark 8:1-10

Twelve is almost always about Israel. Twelve disciples is likely to be about the new Israel. There being twelve baskets of leftover pieces probably indicates that the generosity of God's Kingdom and compassion is always enough to feed and restore Israel.

But, we may ask, why tell us also about a similar event with different numbers?

Perhaps the clue is in the equivalent number. Seven is the 'perfect' number; the number of days of creation; the traditional number of 'nations'. So maybe seven baskets of leftover pieces indicates that the compassion and generosity of God's Kingdom is always enough to feed the whole creation: the new creation is for all nations.

This incident of the feeding of the five thousand is unique amongst stories about Jesus (with the exception of his death and resurrection) in being in all four Gospels, but there are differences. This is not the place to look at all of them but two are instructive.

We've already noticed that Mark's account sets it in the context of Jesus' remark about the people being *"like sheep without a shepherd"*. There's also an extra word in Mark's account when Jesus gets the people to sit down. Mark says that the grass they sat on was *"green"*.

This is one of only three words of colour in Mark's Gospel. Combine this with the sheep saying and with feeding and being in Jesus' presence and it begins to look like a fulfilment of Psalm 23:

The Lord is my shepherd, I lack nothing.
He makes me lie down in green pastures,
He leads me beside quiet waters,
He refreshes my soul.
...
You prepare a table before me
...
Surely your goodness and love will follow me
All the days of my life,
And I will dwell in the house of the Lord forever.

Another difference about Matthew's account from the amalgam idea of the story that we tend to have in our heads is that you might have noticed there's something missing. In case you haven't missed him, the character who isn't there is the small boy who produced the loaves and fishes.

There are a number of reasons why Matthew may not have mentioned him. It may be that he simply forgot; it may be that he's not in Mark either and Matthew didn't trouble to think back but just used Mark's account as the basis for his; it may be that Matthew never knew he was there in the first place. It is John who tells us about him and about Andrew bringing him to Jesus. There's a significance in that if we were looking at John's account – but we're not!

Our question is, "What is Matthew doing by not putting him in?" In other words, what is Matthew saying by telling it the way he does?

"They don't have to leave," answered Jesus. "You yourselves give them something to eat!"

"All we have here are five loaves and two fish," they replied.

"Then bring them here to me," Jesus said.[5]

You yourselves give them something to eat.

Remember, this is not just answering a question of what happened on a particular occasion just after John the Baptist was beheaded.

Why does Matthew want us to hear that Jesus told his disciples to give them something to eat?

He's come to restore God's people, to establish the things of God's Kingdom among God's people; God's people are to do what God does; God has compassion and pity for those in need – he heals their sick, and he also feeds the hungry. God's people don't send away the needy and the hungry; they have pity and they feed them.

But how are God's people to fulfil their role when they have so little?

"All we have here are five loaves and two fish." ...

"...bring them here to me," Jesus said.

What's that all about?

Well, I hope we've got the idea now. We're looking not so much at what happened as what it's all about; it's about what Matthew's readers are to conclude about themselves and their own place among Jesus' followers. That's what he's really trying to convey.

---

[5] Matthew 14:16-18

So this is what we notice as we read it, as it is likely that Matthew's readers have noticed for nearly twenty centuries:

- We bring ourselves – but all we have is…
- We bring what little we think of ourselves.
- We bring what little difference we think we can make.
- We bring the meagre resources of ourselves.

And what he does is:

- take it;
- give thanks for it;
- break it; and
- give it back for them to distribute.

Take it, give thanks, break it and distribute it.
Four actions: take, give thanks, break, distribute.
You might recognise that. It sounds a bit like communion. You see it at any communion service when we take bread, give thanks for it, break it and distribute it.

In John's account of this event it is even more explicit because he attaches a long speech to the event and Jesus talks about the bread of life and giving his body for food. We'll look at that in chapter 19.[6]

Matthew's account makes a subtler reference, but remembering that we're in a lonely place and people have come out of the towns might remind us of Moses feeding the people in the wilderness after the Exodus as God's people are being formed on their journey to the Promised Land. Perhaps Matthew's point is that Jesus' followers are to form the new Israel, God's renewed people.

Bring that up to date and put ourselves in the position of Jesus' followers who read Matthew's Gospel and it describes our role and our actions:

- We offer ourselves – what little we are and what little we think we have.
- He takes us and he gives thanks – we are more than we might think!
- He breaks us – it is seldom an easy ride to offer ourselves in God's service, but the result is that we are given back to

---

[6] Jesus on Memorable Meals (i)

ourselves and we can make a difference beyond anything we could have imagined.

There are two ways we can read this, and both are important to take away from a sermon.

There is both encouragement and challenge.

First the challenge:

Are you ready to offer yourself?

- It doesn't matter what resources you think you have.
- It doesn't matter how little you think you have to offer.
- It doesn't matter if you think your gifts don't amount to very much.

What matters is that you offer it, that you give yourself to be broken and used in his service to make a difference for the Kingdom because he will take whatever you are, whatever you offer and in his hands you can be and do more than you can imagine. Offer yourself in God's service to feed the hungry, to raise up the least, bring to prominence the last and seek the lost.

That's the challenge: offer yourself.

But there is also encouragement:

- Look at what you are and what you have already offered.
- Look at your church and its people and see the difference that can be made.

Look at the number of people you have contact with through the activities that take place and the ways in which you already offer yourselves as a church community.

Don't write off the little that you are and the little that you do. In his hands it can make a difference beyond anything you can imagine.

In one of the churches where I preach, they had a Strawberry Tea the day before looking at this passage. They didn't quite feed five thousand people with tea and scones (though there was almost enough cream for five thousand) but they touched quite a large number of people. Those people all came into the church building; some of them took an opportunity to go into the church for a few moments' quiet; their donations helped a large number more through the charity that was supported by the event; their conversations helped to build relationships and extend a welcome and hospitality to the community.

Be encouraged that what you already offer can go a long way when you put it into his hands; and be challenged continually to offer what little you have because when you put it into his hands, it can do more than you can ask or imagine.

2

Jesus on Fasting (i)

Temptations

Luke 4:1-13

Jesus, full of the Holy Spirit, left the Jordan and was led by the Spirit into the wilderness, where for forty days he was tempted by the devil. He ate nothing during those days, and at the end of them he was hungry.

The devil said to him, 'If you are the Son of God, tell this stone to become bread.'

Jesus answered, 'It is written: "Man shall not live on bread alone."'

The devil led him up to a high place and showed him in an instant all the kingdoms of the world. And he said to him, 'I will give you all their authority and splendour; it has been given to me, and I can give it to anyone I want to. If you worship me, it will all be yours.'

Jesus answered, 'It is written: "Worship the Lord your God and serve him only."'

The devil led him to Jerusalem and had him stand on the highest point of the temple. 'If you are the Son of God,' he said, 'throw yourself down from here. For it is written: "He will command his angels concerning you to guard you carefully; they will lift you up in their hands, so that you will not strike your foot against a stone."'

Jesus answered, 'It is said: "Do not put the Lord your God to the test."'

When the devil had finished all this tempting, he left him until an opportune time.

When our children were small, we could tell when it was coming time for a meal or a snack because their behaviour changed. As their blood sugar levels dropped, their ability to concentrate and make sensible decisions also diminished. As I get older, I notice something similar in me though I hope I can control it better. Diabetics know better than most the dangers of allowing their blood sugar levels to drop. For those reasons, fasting as one of the spiritual disciplines is something to be considered very carefully.

Fasting can be a very positive experience that concentrates the mind on what the body actually needs rather than what we want or seems to be an attractive prospect. Eating nothing for forty days is taking fasting to extreme and is probably bad for all of us – even if forty days is not literally nearly six weeks but just 'a long time'.

This passage is often read at the beginning of Lent – a period of forty days' preparation for Easter beginning on Ash Wednesday. Readers with an in-built calendar will have realised already that there are forty-six days between Ash Wednesday and Easter Day. The conclusion is that Sunday is always a feast day (even in Lent) because it is the day of resurrection. So, even if you fast for the whole of Lent, you can eat on Sundays – or eat whatever it is that you've 'given up for Lent'. Even so, six days without eating at all is a long time.

The Bible contains many understatements and one of them comes near the beginning of this passage. *"He ate nothing during those [forty] days, and at the end of them he was hungry."*[7] I expect he was!

---

[7] Luke 4:2

And being hungry he was vulnerable. It looks as though Jesus had deliberately put himself in that position. It looks as though Jesus' fasting at this point just after the high point and affirmation at his baptism was in order to work something out. From what Luke has said in the first three chapters of his Gospel, it looks as though what Jesus needed to work out was exactly what his vocation as 'Son of God' might mean and just how he was to go about inheriting the *"throne of his father David"* and becoming the one who would *"reign over the house of Jacob for ever"*.[8]

Fasting can concentrate the mind in a very positive way but it also has the result of making us hungry. Luke shows from the genealogy that immediately precedes this passage[9] and from Jesus' hunger that Jesus was a human being. He has also shown that in many ways he is no ordinary human being but fully human with a very high calling and purpose derived from his also being not just descended from Adam but also Son of God.

As we read the Bible the devil always seems personal and that can be a helpful focus, but it can also help us to dodge some personal issues because we don't meet the devil in a personal way. If we see Jesus' encounter with the devil as the voice of temptation in his head coming from the accumulated human tendency to wander away from the path of obedience to God, to make a mess of our relationships and to have an inflated view of our own importance, then we can associate with the episode more easily.

There are three 'temptations' in this account. The first derives directly from fasting by going without food for a long time. Jesus was hungry and the temptation was that if he was 'Son of God', as God declared at his baptism, then he could feed himself from the stones that lay around him.

The simplest level of interpretation of this could be that when we've been fasting, it is tempting to think that a biscuit with our glass of water mid-morning that no one knows about won't matter. I think it would be simplistic, and a wrong use of the Bible, to say that 'we don't live on biscuits alone, we need coffee and cake as well'! There must be something else to it.

---

[8] Luke 1:32-33
[9] Luke 3:23-38

So, rather than attempt to go through each temptation separately, let's take them together as aspects of one thing. Jesus is fasting as part of a retreat at the beginning of his ministry while he works out the nature of his vocation as declared by the voice from heaven at his baptism, *"You are my Son, whom I love; with you I am well pleased."*[10]

Each of the temptations appear in his head as plausible, attractive answers to the question of how he fulfils this God-given vocation and they make a lot of sense. God can't want the son whom he loves to die of starvation – or even be as hungry as you would be after forty days without food. If he's meant to reign over the whole world then if there's an easy way to achieve that, why not go for it? And as Israel's Messiah, surely pulling off a spectacular stunt to prove it would help in his acceptance?

When we read of temptation we tend to think of Adam and Eve in the garden and plausible lies about what God actually said and what that might really have meant. Jesus meets that aspect head on and overcomes Adam and Eve's fall by quoting from Deuteronomy to show up the devil's duplicity. There is reference here to Adam and Eve but there is more to it than that. Jesus is to be Israel's liberator and so bring true freedom for all. It would be surprising if there were not references to the nature of Israel's rebellion against God. And so there are.

At the Exodus Israel was freed from Egypt and declared to be God's son. During forty years of wandering in the wilderness, Israel grumbled about food and demanded bread; they also set up an idol in the form of a golden calf to worship in place of God and continually tested God.

Put like that, I hope the parallels are obvious. At his baptism in the Jordan, Jesus was declared to be God's beloved son and now for forty days in the wilderness he is working out how he can live up to that and bring true liberation for Israel and the world.

As with all vocations, the answer starts with the personal. The secret biscuit with a glass of water mid-morning while supposedly fasting will make the more public disciplines much harder. The public person is formed by the Spirit working internally and privately.

---

[10] Luke 3:22

Similarly, Jesus is formed for his public ministry in the privacy of his personal wrestling with temptation in the wilderness. The story of Israel shows how the nation had struggled and failed with similar tests; the story of Jesus will show how he struggled and overcame them.

Physical needs are important: the diabetic should not attempt to fast beyond their capacity. But Jesus shows that loyalty and obedience to God and being formed as a child of God is even more important.

Jesus will become the Lord and ruler of the world but the route to that position and the way it is exercised are not the ways of status and power which the world expects but through humble service.

Trust in God is supremely important but deliberately putting himself into harm's way to force God into a spectacular rescue stunt is not trust but seeks prestige and his own reputation.

Jesus' rule which inaugurates God's reign is through a use of his power that brings healing, inclusion and hope to the broken, marginalised and despairing. Jesus' humble service rather than spectacular showmanship will bring light and life rather than darkness and death.

What Jesus says about fasting is that it is an opportunity to focus on our vocation as God's beloved children and its basis in God's promises which we find in the Bible. When that is tested by insidious but plausible and attractive lies, we will then be able to recognise them, distinguish them from the voice of God and access the words of truth.

What Jesus says about fasting, through his own experience, is that it is a discipline that enables us to celebrate our full humanity as God's children called to follow Jesus in the path to glory which lies in life in all its fullness.

3

Jesus on Fishing

Let Your Nets Down for a Catch

Luke 5:1-11

One day as Jesus was standing by the Lake of Gennesaret, the people were crowding round him and listening to the word of God. He saw at the water's edge two boats, left there by the fishermen, who were washing their nets. He got into one of the boats, the one belonging to Simon, and asked him to put out a little from the shore. Then he sat down and taught the people from the boat. When he had finished speaking, he said to Simon, 'Put out into deep water, and let down the nets for a catch.'

Simon answered, 'Master, we've worked hard all night and haven't caught anything. But because you say so, I will let down the nets.'

When they had done so, they caught such a large number of fish that their nets began to break. So they signalled to their partners in the other boat to come and help them, and they came and filled both boats so full that they began to sink. When Simon Peter saw this, he fell at Jesus' knees and said, 'Go away from me, Lord; I am a sinful man!' For he and all his companions were astonished at the catch of fish they had taken, and so were James and John, the sons of Zebedee, Simon's partners.

Then Jesus said to Simon, 'Don't be afraid; from now on you will fish for people.' So they pulled their boats up on shore, left everything and followed him.

This story in any other place would read as simply a hungry carpenter turned preacher demonstrating his ignorance about fishing practices.

Let's start by being clear exactly what happened before we look at what it's all about.

The time must be getting on through the morning. The fishermen who had been out at night were washing their nets. It looks as though they'd had a catch of weed and other detritus from the lake but no fish. There has been enough time for a crowd to gather to listen to Jesus, the new travelling preacher who had come from Nazareth. Jesus knew enough about speaking to a crowd to understand that his voice would carry better over water than he was finding being hemmed in between the crowd and the water line. The boat on the shore was an obvious solution.

So far so good. But Luke must have recorded this for a better reason than to demonstrate a simple matter of physics. The tips to be gained about fishing are misleading as it turned out that all the established procedures for successful fishing were broken but the fishing was phenomenally successful.

As usual Jesus uses an everyday occurrence to make a deeper point. So what is it all about?

It looks as though Jesus is taking Simon through a number of stages in his thinking and their developing relationship. He starts by asking for some help. He wonders if Simon might be available to give him assistance by achieving that distance from the crowd so that people could hear him as he exploits the natural amphitheatre of the bays along that part of the lake.

Simon's willingness might have stemmed from an excuse to put off the net-washing for a while, but it meant he was a captive audience. If the people on the shore could hear Jesus, Simon could certainly hear him in the boat. It is possible that it took some effort on Simon's part to hold the boat steady while Jesus spoke. Simon would have been concentrating. We're not told what Jesus said but it was likely to be on the same lines as most of his teaching. It would have been about the way God rules and how people can be part of that. The style would have been accessible to his hearers using examples they could identify with and it would have had the air of authority that comes across when someone knows what they're talking about.

Maybe Jesus had been watching Simon as he spoke and saw that he had been listening. Or maybe Jesus had identified Simon previously as someone he wanted to recruit. However it came about, when Jesus finished speaking he came to the second stage of developing his relationship with Simon.

"Put out into deep water, and let down the nets for a catch."

This is where Jesus ignores all accepted procedures for fishing – or demonstrates ignorance of them. They had been out all night and were washing the nets. This is not the time to suggest fishing – especially not if you're a carpenter and you're talking to a professional fisherman. It is not surprising that Simon protests. What is surprising is that we see how far his relationship with Jesus has developed during that morning in the boat. He recognises someone who not only has some interesting things to say but speaks with authority – perhaps about unexpected subjects.

The second part of Simon's response indicates that he recognises leadership and authority:

"...because you say so, I will let down the nets."

As a fisherman Jesus had all the beginner's luck. First time out at the wrong time of the day just after a failed night and he gets such a catch that the nets began to break and even with another boat to help they began to sink.

You can understand Simon's reaction to send Jesus away. Here he is, not only showing him up as a fisherman but potentially ruining his business by sinking his boats with all the fish. It looks ironic that after failure might have left them hungry, success might have sunk the business altogether. No wonder Simon says, *"Go away from me..."*

No doubt you're ahead of me. That's not quite what he said, is it? Simon didn't go up to Jesus and threaten him or shout at him to,

"Get out of my boat!" The tone is altogether different. Simon fell at Jesus' knees and said, *"Go away from me, Lord; I am a sinful man!"*

They were astonished at the catch of fish, but they weren't marvelling at Jesus' mysterious expertise. It had made them aware of something about themselves. There are two words that have become technical terms in Simon's response and put their relationship in perspective. Simon calls Jesus *"Lord"* as he recognises his power and authority. This is no ordinary person if everything is reversed with such dramatic effect. Simon's failure of a night's fishing is turned to overwhelming success at the wrong time of day. Only an awesome power could achieve that. His feelings are of respect and fear.

Simon also sees himself in perspective – *"I am a sinful man!"* He sees the way he makes a mess of his relationships; perhaps he sees how he has made a mess of the previous night's fishing; perhaps he thinks there might have been reasons why they caught nothing that were down to him; perhaps he realised he had been less than gracious in his agreement for the use of his boat. Whatever the specifics, he knows that he's not as good as he likes to think.

But Jesus hasn't finished with him and this is where it comes home to us as well. When Jesus calls – when Jesus gets someone in his sights and pursues the relationship – he doesn't give up. Effectively Jesus to Simon, "From now on we're going into partnership. It's not about fish; forget these little tiddlers even if there are a lot of them. From now on it's about people. Come with me and go after the six-foot varieties."

As usual there's something going on behind what happens. This looks like fishing, it sounds like fishing; no doubt at the time it smelt like fishing. But it's not really about fishing.

There are many people – perhaps including many who read this – who can put themselves in Simon's position. Simon – later known as Peter and referred to part way through Luke's account here as Simon Peter – is the disciple more people associate with than any other.

Simon Peter makes mistakes; he opens his mouth and puts his foot in it; he has great enthusiasm and insight but doesn't think it through; he lies to get himself out of a tight spot that he's got himself into through his loyalty.

Many of us can put ourselves in Simon's position and realise that we have been called and find we have no option but to give everything and go with him when we have no idea what it might lead to. It is scary but compelling; we know it was not a question. It was not, "How about you come along with me for a bit and see how it goes?" It was a command: "From now on you will fish for people."

But many people can't quite put themselves in that position. Maybe you see yourself on the shore watching this unusual fishing expedition after the preacher has finished speaking from the boat. If you're reading this, you've heard enough to think there must be something going on with Jesus and perhaps you've seen other people's lives changed but maybe you're not ready to jump in with both feet, let down your net for a catch or jump out of your boat and go off leaving everything behind while you follow Jesus into unknown territory.

But Luke tells the story for a reason. This is not just about how Peter came from being Simon the fisherman to Peter the Apostle. The reason Simon and his partners were called was so that Jesus' message of the coming to earth of God's rule in the same way as it is in heaven would spread wider and wider. Luke intends to show us that it is by responding to that call that lives change and become more like the Kingdom of God. Effectively he's saying we may as well take the bait because we're all fish in God's sea and we're all fishermen in God's boat and God doesn't want anyone left out.

4

Jesus on the Guest List

The Calling of Matthew

Matthew 9:9-13

As Jesus went on from there, he saw a man named Matthew sitting at the tax collector's booth. 'Follow me,' he told him, and Matthew got up and followed him.

While Jesus was having dinner at Matthew's house, many tax collectors and sinners came and ate with him and his disciples. When the Pharisees saw this, they asked his disciples, 'Why does your teacher eat with tax collectors and sinners?'

On hearing this, Jesus said, 'It is not the healthy who need a doctor, but those who are ill. But go and learn what this means: "I desire mercy, not sacrifice." For I have not come to call the righteous, but sinners.'

Lots of people have parties to celebrate changes in their circumstances, or when they make a transition from one phase of life to another. The obvious one is a wedding reception when a couple celebrate their marriage by having friends and family together from all aspects of their lives: families from each side, friends of the groom and friends of the bride as well as friends that they've made together.

It's an occasion that looks back as well as looking forward in celebration with hope and expectation.

It looks as though Matthew has understood this idea. Traditionally, this is Matthew's account of his own calling to follow Jesus. It's a point of dramatic transition in his life. He goes from being a tax collector to a follower of Jesus. Let's get the obvious difficulty in interpretation out of the way early. Being a tax collector in first century Palestine was not the same as working for Her Majesty's Revenue and Customs in twenty-first century Britain.

Matthew would have been unpopular with his contemporaries for his collaboration with the occupying forces of Rome and for the way in which he would have overcharged in order to make a living for himself. Some did this to such an extent that they became very wealthy themselves. The unpopularity became even more pointed as people moved from one area or province to another and the transaction had to take place. There was no Dart Charge or ability to pay online; you had to deal personally with the person in the booth without the safety of a car. It would have been a personal encounter across a table while the tax collector sat in his booth and you counted out the necessary coins to continue on your way.

Interestingly, Matthew tells us that Jesus simply *told* him to follow him. It is not a question or an invitation. It is not, "How would it be if you came along with me for a bit and see how you like a different way of life?" It is a command: *"Follow me."*

As so often, the little words are worth looking at in this passage. Matthew tells us that in response to Jesus' instruction to follow him, he *"got up and followed him"*. The words for *"got up"* have been chosen carefully. It's not simply a description that he stood up, or that he left the booth like the fishermen left their nets, and it doesn't just say that Matthew *went* with Jesus. The word for *"got up"* might better be translated 'arose' – a word often used in connection with resurrection. By using that word, Matthew slips in a sense of how dramatic a change of life this was. It makes it similar to being raised from the dead.

This is where our first tool of interpretation comes in useful. It looks as though that might be one reason why Matthew places the account of his calling where he does, between the healing of a paralysed man who was instructed to, *"Get up, take your mat and go home,"*[11] and before visiting Jairus's daughter who had just died. Jesus *"took the girl by the hand, and she <u>got up</u>"*[12].

Becoming a follower of Jesus is such a change in lifestyle and direction that Matthew lets us know he had to celebrate by holding a party. He also tells us who was on his guest list. When people leave a job either to move on to another or when they retire, the party is usually at the workplace or nearby and those invited might include some close family but it is principally for former colleagues.

Matthew has invited his former colleagues to this party. In some ways it looks like a party that looks back at what he's leaving. But it isn't described that way. It is looking forward to something new. Matthew moves straight from describing that dramatic new beginning to dinner at Matthew's house:

"While Jesus was having dinner at Matthew's house..."[13]

The emphasis is on a new beginning with Jesus. Matthew has left his tax collecting but he hasn't left his home. This is a party to celebrate the beginning of his following Jesus – not the end of his tax-collecting career. But many tax collectors and sinners came and ate with him as well.

To draw a ministry parallel, it looks more like a party after an Anglican Induction service than after a Methodist Welcome service. A Methodist Welcome will be almost entirely people from the receiving Circuit where a minister is just starting. That is partly because the Circuit the minister has come from will be very likely to be having a similar event for a new minister themselves.

An Anglican Induction service is likely to be attended by a contingent from the minister's former parish. There's a mixture of the 'old' and the 'new' so people from the new parish get to meet and talk with people from the old. No doubt they swap stories of their experiences. It is similar to a wedding reception where the two families that come together through the couple getting married speak to each other and swap stories and experiences of the one they know best and friends of both hear from other friends and relatives who know one or another better.

---

[11] Matthew 9:6
[12] Emphasis added
[13] Matthew 9:10

As we get to verse eleven, we might wonder where the Pharisees sprung from all of a sudden. They don't seem to fit either category. They're not former colleagues and associates of a tax collector and they're not among Jesus' followers either. It reminds us that these events would have been more or less in public, in a courtyard of a house where passers-by might be able to stand by the wall. Pharisees who might have been keeping an eye on Jesus to see what he got up to would have noticed who was at the party. They were not concerned about who Matthew invited to dinner. Presumably a tax collector inviting others to dinner was commonplace and not particularly frowned upon. It would also have been unremarkable that other 'sinners' – people who, for one reason or another, were outside the strict Jewish interpretations of acceptability – were also invited. What the Pharisees couldn't understand was that Jesus would mix with such company if he was a Jewish teacher with a developing reputation as one who was going to restore Israel and bring freedom to God's people. Such a person should keep himself pure and holy and not mix with the undesirables.

Jesus' comments on the guest list for Matthew's party are instructive about his role and how he saw himself. And they also speak to us about who is on the guest list for our parties.

Jesus sees himself less in terms of purity and holiness as a means to God's favour and the establishment of his rule, and more in terms of health and healing. He says that the sick will not get better if you simply leave them to themselves to mix only with other sick people. It's all very well having sick people in hospital but unless you also have some doctors and some nurses and other healthy people there to treat them, they won't recover. And a doctor spending all his or her time with people who are healthy will be a waste of their training and abilities and not fulfil their vocation.[14]

Mark tells the same story, giving Matthew the name Levi. But Matthew inserts a reference to the prophet Hosea[15] for the benefit of his mostly Jewish Christian community. It further emphasises the placing of this account among a series of healings. Jesus was getting a name as a person who brought health and healing, having mercy on

---

[14] Mark 2:13-17
[15] Hosea 6:6 quoted by Jesus in Matthew 9:13, "I desire mercy not sacrifice."

the sick and the marginalised. Matthew's call and the example of Jesus going to eat with him, his former colleagues in the tax collecting community and other 'sinners', is a demonstration of practical mercy for the outcast.

It demonstrates that Jesus' approach of bringing practical help to the sick, the poor, the marginalised and the despised was having a greater impact in terms of bringing the life and light of God into dark and despairing lives than the whole system of the Temple with its sacrifices and demands for ritual purity.

Jesus ends the discussion by saying, *"I have not come to call the righteous, but sinners."* It would be legitimate to ask, *"Who are the righteous?"* and we might expect that if there are any at all, the Pharisees don't truly fit the description. That leaves us with a sense of Jesus' irony. But there's more to Matthew's party than another piece in the jigsaw of how Jesus saw himself. It also helps us with the guest list for our own parties.

Matthew invited his old friends and former colleagues as well as Jesus and his new friends and fellow followers. How much do we not only allow but encourage different parts of our lives to mix?

When we have a birthday party, do we invite people only from work or from family or from our friends at church or the Horticultural Society or whatever other organisation we spend our time with? Or do we invite people from all sections of our lives?

If we're baptised or confirmed as an adult, do we invite colleagues from work and friends from the Bridge Club and the Ramblers Group as well as our new home group at church and those who helped us to discover what following Jesus can be about today?

If you've 'got up' and know that life is different because you follow Jesus, why not have a 'Matthew party' and invite people from all parts of your life along with your Christian friends and sit back, enjoy the food and drink and company, and watch what happens when they discover one another, their backgrounds and connections?

5

Jesus on Fasting (ii)

Jesus is Questioned about Fasting

Mark 2:18-22

Now John's disciples and the Pharisees were fasting. Some people came and asked Jesus, 'How is it that John's disciples and the disciples of the Pharisees are fasting, but yours are not?'

Jesus answered, 'How can the guests of the bridegroom fast while he is with them? They cannot, so long as they have him with them. But the time will come when the bridegroom will be taken from them, and on that day they will fast.

'No one sews a patch of unshrunk cloth on an old garment. Otherwise, the new piece will pull away from the old, making the tear worse. And no one pours new wine into old wineskins. Otherwise, the wine will burst the skins, and both the wine and the wineskins will be ruined. No, they pour new wine into new wineskins.'

Jesus was asked why he and his disciples were not fasting when the Pharisees and the disciples of John the Baptist were fasting. Before we look at the answer – what Jesus had to say about fasting –

it might be an idea to ask why the Pharisees and John and his disciples were fasting.

As with traditional Christian fast periods and the Muslim fast in Ramadan, Jews fasted on particular occasions as a discipline to remind them of something in their relationship with God. Some Christians fast (or at least eat more simply) on a Friday as a reminder of Jesus' death on Good Friday. Many have some discipline of 'giving something up' for Lent as a reminder of Jesus' fast in preparation for his ministry after his baptism.[16] Jews of the first century fasted mainly on days to remind them of the great disasters of the past. An example would be a day of fasting to commemorate the destruction of the Temple in 587BC. A modern parallel would be for the French to fast in May as a reminder of the invasion in May 1940. We tend to do things on a smaller scale. Rather than the whole nation standing in silence, the families or communities most involved keep a silence or period of solemnity to remember particular disasters.[17]

That gives us some clue to the background to the question posed to Jesus about fasting. Surely he would want to mark these holy days? Surely a devout Jew with a growing reputation for teaching the ways of God in a similar vein to John the Baptist would want to mark these solemn times as a reminder of the ways God's people had gone wrong in the past? These past disasters were seen as times when the nation had been punished for their failure and infidelity in being God's holy people. Surely it was right to look back with repentance and fasting?

All that sounds plausible, but Jesus' answer is no.

Fortunately for us as we try to interpret his answer and wonder whether it has anything to say to us, Jesus gives three typically vivid but contemporary illustrations. Let's try to bring them up to date without losing the sense Jesus would have conveyed to his original hearers.

Stemming from the question about fasting, Jesus starts by asking us to think of a wedding. Weddings take a lot of planning and

---

[16] See chapter 2

[17] Just one example would be that on the day I am writing, families are remembering loved ones who died when a vintage aircraft crashed on a road during an air show two years ago. There are always likely to be up-to-date or timely examples.

preparation these days. Presumably the details and practicalities were different then but would still have involved a good deal of preparation. Jesus is saying that when you're planning events like that, you don't try to combine a wedding with a particularly solemn occasion for the family. You don't hold a wedding and a funeral on the same day. You can't expect a happy couple and their family and friends to stop their celebrations to have two minutes' silence in commemoration of a historic national disaster.

Tom Wright tells of a letter to the *Times* in which a man describes how he got married in Lent but did it on a Sunday so there still could be a feast.[18] Sunday is the day of resurrection and new life so the Sundays in Lent don't count as part of the forty days of fasting – count them up some time and rejoice that on the Sundays you can have that piece of chocolate or whatever you gave up for Lent!

What Jesus is saying about fasting in his own day is that his presence is like being at a wedding and you can't expect the guests to sit round looking miserable and not touching the food. Jesus uses the example of a wedding because it was (and still is) a good way of talking about the love and goodness and creativity of God who makes all things new where there is plenty for everyone and justice and peace for all.

There's also a sense that by describing himself as the bridegroom, Jesus is referring to Israel as God's bride and reminding them of their past infidelities and rebellions just as the fasting was meant to do. Maybe if the bridegroom is present reminding them of their past failures, the coming wrath that John the Baptist mentioned might not be so far off. It should at least give pause for thought and reflection.

The second image Jesus uses is about mending clothes. Perhaps this is 'Jesus on needlework' rather than food but it goes with the other two. The point that is not being made (which you could conclude from this illustration on its own) is that the old is better than the new. All analogies break down at some point – even Jesus'. Very simply Jesus is leading to his final illustration and saying that the old and the new don't mix. When you put them together, the results are unfortunate. In this example an old and much-loved garment that needs mending ends up with an even worse hole in it.

---

[18] Tom Wright, *Mark for Everyone,* SPCK (2001), p24

The third image about wineskins makes the same point as the image of mending clothes. Now he talks about wine. This seems to be 'Jesus on wine storage'. Maybe he's going to give advice about laying down a good cellar. But no – as usual it is not what he says that's important so much as what he's talking about. Wine and vineyards are always about Israel and always about the way God relates to his people. At the time, wine was kept in skins rather than bottles.

What Jesus is referring to is a container in which much of the process of wine-making happened.

Wine was made by treading barefoot on the grapes in a wine press, from which the juice flowed into a wine vat which functioned as a collecting and fermenting container. In the warm climate of Palestine, grape juice began to ferment very quickly and there was no easy way to prevent it. After the first fermentation had taken place in the vat, the wine was separated from the sediment and strained through a sieve or piece of cloth. After four to six days it was poured into containers – sometimes clay jars lined with pitch but often animal skins for storage and further fermentation; these are the wineskins Jesus refers to.

Wineskins were whole goatskins with the neck tied off where the wine has been poured in. The whole skin would bulge almost to bursting as the carbon dioxide gas generated by the fermentation process stretched it to its limit.

Fermentation in the wineskin would continue until eventually the process slowed down and stopped. By that time the skin would be stretched to its limit. The alcohol is probably about 12%, and this destroys the skin's natural ability to contract and stretch again. Once wine has fermented in a skin, the nature of the skin has changed. Put new wine into it and it has no stretch left and will simply burst with the build-up of gas.

The principle idea that Jesus is working on with both these illustrations is that the old thing – cloth or wineskin – is incapable of holding the new – cloth or wine – because it is not flexible, it won't stretch and expand with the expanding or shrinking of the new.

If you put new wine into the old wineskin that has already stretched to the limit with a previous vintage, the result will be a burst wineskin that is no longer good for anything and, more seriously, spilt wine.

What Jesus is saying is that his presence means that God is doing the new thing that he has promised for so long. This is not the time to be looking back with however much regret or repentance for the failures of the past. Now, Jesus is saying, because of his coming, is the time to be looking forward in celebration of the new ways of God who brings peace and justice, healing and hope; the promise of life renewed and refreshed out of all recognition. That, he says, can't be mixed with the old methods of the world around us or even the religious traditions which have served their useful purpose.

Where it takes courage is to recognise the new things God is doing and join the party rather than agonise over the threat to our old wineskins or moan about the way our old coat has been ruined.

Human beings seem to be naturally religious people; we have to have systems and rules and regulations for how we go about our worship and our festivals and our relationships.

Wineskins are good things to have to contain wine. Without them the wine is wasted. But the wineskins have to be flexible to contain something that is new and alive with fermentation.

This can be about religious structures and traditions, but it is also about us personally. Don't let your religious devotion blind you to Jesus' presence. Look for what is good and living. Look for the good things that Jesus is doing, where he brings life and wholeness. Pursue the devotion, the spiritual disciplines of fasting, prayer, reading the Bible, but more importantly see how Jesus reveals himself in them.

Don't be tempted to return to a system that is simply a system – a rigid system of Law and regulation that can't contain what is of Grace and living and vibrant.

Jesus' advice on fasting is that it is fine as a discipline and a reminder but when the new thing is happening, when the bridegroom is actually here, fasting is inappropriate. When you recognise his presence, join in the celebration and let him pour his new wine into your new wineskins.

6

Jesus on Wine Tasting

The Wedding at Cana

John 2:1-12

On the third day a wedding took place at Cana in Galilee. Jesus' mother was there, and Jesus and his disciples had also been invited to the wedding. When the wine was gone, Jesus' mother said to him, 'They have no more wine.'

'Woman, why do you involve me?' Jesus replied. 'My hour has not yet come.'

His mother said to the servants, 'Do whatever he tells you.'

Nearby stood six stone water jars, the kind used by the Jews for ceremonial washing, each holding from eighty to a hundred and twenty litres. Jesus said to the servants, 'Fill the jars with water'; so they filled them to the brim. Then he told them, 'Now draw some out and take it to the master of the banquet.'

They did so, and the master of the banquet tasted the water that had been turned into wine. He did not realise where it had come from, though the servants who had drawn the water knew. Then he called the bridegroom aside and said, 'Every-

one brings out the choice wine first and then the cheaper wine after the guests have had too much to drink; but you have saved the best till now.'

What Jesus did here in Cana of Galilee was the first of the signs through which he revealed his glory; and his disciples believed in him.

After this he went down to Capernaum with his mother and brothers and his disciples. There they stayed for a few days.

The steward at the wedding banquet obviously knew his wines. He had not over-imbibed and when asked to taste a new bottle that was being presented, he could tell that this wasn't a cheap chateau plonk that the guests would hardly notice. Maybe Jesus' take on wine tasting is that you might come across a gem later in the session so don't overdo it early on. He might be saying that, and it is a message worth hearing, but it's a bit simplistic to find its way into the Bible in the midst of a story with so much symbolism around it.

John has many motifs and symbolic words and phrases that point us towards the truths he wants to convey. More even than with other biblical writers, it is worth looking not just at what happens in John's narrative but also asking, "What's that all about, then?"

So, what is it all about that in order to avoid social disaster at a wedding Jesus turns hundreds of litres of water into the best wine the steward has ever tasted?

There are a number of John's 'signpost' words just in that question but there are even more in the twelve verses it takes him to give his account.

We could start with wine as that seems to be the main subject of this story. We have noticed in the previous chapter when Jesus mentions wine storage that the subject of wine has echoes of Israel and God's work in and for his people. Maybe there's something of that going on in this story.

Another 'signpost' word is when Jesus talks about his 'time' not yet having come. Throughout John's Gospel from this first reference onwards he is pointing forward to Jesus' 'time'. There's a clue to when it might be in the presence of Jesus' mother. The only other time she is present in John's account is at the cross. That's the 'time' when his glory is fully revealed and the moment when heaven and earth fully intersect.

Mary's instruction to the servants to *"do whatever he tells you"* is also a phrase we should note. It doesn't arise often, but its sense is about obedience and noticing what happens when people do what Jesus tells them. When we do whatever he tells us we might notice something.

The next 'signpost' in this story is that John refers to the containers for the water that will be turned into wine. They were the stone water jars used for Jewish purification rites. It is not just that they were handy containers standing nearby. They don't just stand nearby – they stand *for* something. Whatever is going to happen is within and coming out of the old ways – the Jewish ways. What Jesus is about is bringing purification to Israel – and from there to the world – but in completely new ways.

But we need to go back to the wine. That is the main subject of the story and provides the main 'signpost'. The water from the jars used for purification was turned into wine. It was changed, renewed, given a new life in celebration and feasting. Just as the water was transformed into wine, so the occasion was transformed from catastrophe to celebration.

Running out of wine at a wedding banquet that probably involved the whole village and some from other places too was not just inconvenient requiring an emergency trip to the late-night supermarket. It was a social disaster. From this time on Jesus turns his attention to other kinds of issues but this is a sign of the compassion he shows to people in any kind of need to transform their problems in unexpected ways.

So, it's not good enough simply to ask what happened. And to ask, as some do, whether it's possible is the wrong question. The first point is that something happened or we wouldn't have the accounts of the events. The second point is that it must have been more than conjuring or 'magic' for it to have inspired the faith and transformed the lives of countless millions for centuries afterwards.

The miracles that John recounts, he calls 'signs' because they point us towards a truth; a truth about Jesus as to who he was and what his presence meant. But they also point to a truth about us and our times and what his presence can mean now.

So a good question to ask might be, "What is this sign showing us?" What is turning water into wine at a wedding in Cana in Galilee twenty centuries ago all about now? We've seen some clues that nudge us towards some answers to that but let's go round the event again and see what else we can find. The first tool of interpretation is always context. So, what's the context of this story?

The passage immediately before is the calling of Nathaniel who is invited by Philip to *"come and see"* for himself the Jesus he has been told about. Nathaniel's faith is stimulated by Jesus' knowledge of him, but it is Jesus' promise of what he will see that is important in this context.

Jesus told him that he and the others with him would *"see 'heaven open, and the angels of God ascending and descending on' the Son of Man."*[19] It is a direct reference to Genesis 28 and Jacob's dream in which he saw heaven open and the angels going up and down a ladder whose foot was on earth and top in the heavens. By putting that immediately before his account of the first 'sign', John is signalling that what Jesus' followers will see in Jesus is the meeting point of heaven and earth – that earth and heaven merge in him.

It is worth a brief digression here into what Jesus meant by picking on an otherwise obscure title from Daniel chapter 7 as his favourite way to refer to himself. We tend to get used to it with Jesus, but it would sound odd for anyone else to refer to themselves continually in the third person instead of saying "I" or "me". In Daniel's vision in Daniel chapter 7, the Son of Man is the figure who is raised into God's presence to reign with God in heaven over all the earth when the earthly beasts are defeated. The title 'Son of Man' also seems to be about the contact between earth and heaven, when earth will be subject to God's rule.

There's another clue to the same thing at the beginning of chapter 2. It is worth remembering that John didn't divide his book into chapters. That has very usefully been done by later editors to help us find our way around. Unfortunately, it tends to divide it up in our minds into separated chunks.

---

[19] John 1:51

Immediately after Jesus' promise that his followers would see *"heaven open"* and refers to himself as *"Son of Man"*, John introduces the first 'sign' by saying *"On the third day..."*[20].

That's another 'signpost' phrase for John. I hope you're ahead of me, but I'll spell it out any way. When we read that, we're meant to think of another 'third day' at the end of the Gospel – the day of resurrection. The third day is the day of transformation and change, new life, and the establishment of Jesus' rule over all things. That's what this sign points towards. He can transform and renew the social disaster of a wedding which ran out of wine; he can transform and renew the fears for their future of a family and a couple who have under-catered. In later signs he will transform hunger, despair, blindness and death with food and hope and vision and new life in all its fullness.

This sign points to that which is found in and through and because of Jesus. And let's remember that it is not just an historical account of something that happened and was relevant in first century Palestine. We read it now because it continued to be true and continued to point to the same thing for those who have followed Jesus ever since: those who read these signs and see what Nathaniel saw. He realised that earth and heaven combine and the Son of Man is raised to rule over all so that we may all be raised with him in the new heaven and the new earth of the new creation.

But that is running on ahead. Let's go back to the context of this story and find something else that reinforces what we think John is doing. We have noticed what comes before John chapter 2 (the answer is John chapter 1 – not a trick question, or even testing biblical knowledge!) But what comes after John 2:12?

Answer: John 2:13. It is no accident that John goes straight to his account of Jesus' attendance at the Temple at Passover and his overturning of the symbols of the sacrificial system. The Temple was the place in the Jewish system where earth and heaven met; it was the place for the focus of the presence of God on earth. John is telling us the same message in the episode after the changing of water for purification into wine for celebration. The one we're dealing with

---

[20] John 2:1

here is the focus for the presence of God on earth; this man is the point at which earth and heaven meet.

So, what can we say for ourselves?

Jesus is still the focus for the presence of God on earth. What Jesus is still about is establishing his rule on earth in the same way as it is in heaven. By his Spirit living in and through his people, the Word is still made flesh. Disaster, despair and death are still transformed into triumph, hope and life when we *"do whatever he tells you"* and watch the unexpected transformation.

7

Jesus on Menu Planning?

Do Not Worry About What You Will Eat

Matthew 6:25-34

'Therefore I tell you, do not worry about your life, what you will eat or drink; or about your body, what you will wear. Is not life more than food, and the body more than clothes? Look at the birds of the air; they do not sow or reap or store away in barns, and yet your heavenly Father feeds them. Are you not much more valuable than they? Can any one of you by worrying add a single hour to your life?

'And why do you worry about clothes? See how the flowers of the field grow. They do not labour or spin. Yet I tell you that not even Solomon in all his splendour was dressed like one of these. If that is how God clothes the grass of the field, which is here today and tomorrow is thrown into the fire, will he not much more clothe you – you of little faith? So do not worry, saying, "What shall we eat?" or "What shall we drink?" or "What shall we wear?" For the pagans run after all these things, and your heavenly Father knows that you need them. But seek first his kingdom and his righteousness, and all these things will be given to you as well. Therefore do not worry

about tomorrow, for tomorrow will worry about itself. Each day has enough trouble of its own.'

It is sometimes helpful to think about what shape the sermon has. It would take too long to explain many, but the usual 'shape' is probably a linear walk with certain landmarks on the way in the form of the classic three points that get us from introduction to conclusion. You might have noticed that not many in this collection take that shape!

To continue the walking analogy alongside the idea of shape, sometimes the shape is more of a ramble without a clear idea of beginning and ending or what to notice on the way. Sometimes the ramble is more focussed looking only at aspects relevant to our purpose.

The chapters in Matthew's Gospel known as 'The Sermon on the Mount' are interesting in terms of shape. I have thought for some time that the shape is something of a loop. You start going round the loop at the beginning of chapter 6 and come out of it at the beginning of chapter 7. Chapter 6 contains many helpful and important passages but it would be possible to go straight on from the end of chapter 5 into chapter 7.

After a series of examples about the fulfilment of the law and how its interpretation should be even more strict than it sounds because it relates to the attitudes within and not just outward actions, Jesus poses his greatest challenge:

"Be perfect, therefore, as your heavenly Father is perfect."[21]

It is not a great leap to go on, *"Do not judge, or you too will be judged."*[22] It sounds like an aspect of being perfect. The thing with the loop, when a sermon takes that shape, is that you could leave it out without losing too much of the message or you could just use the loop and still have a message with important points in it. So it is with Matthew chapter 6. It could stand on its own. Or indeed each part of it could be on its own. It's just that they all gain from being part of the whole. Once again it comes down to context.

You could take this passage on its own as a loop in a sermon that has a message all to itself.

---

[21] Matthew 5:38
[22] Matthew 7:1

"Do not worry about your life, what you will eat or drink; or about your body, what you will wear ... your heavenly Father knows that you need them ... each day has enough trouble of its own."

It could be 'Jesus on dietary requirements'. Maybe he's saying, "Don't worry about it; it'll all be OK. God knows your needs and will make sure you don't get nuts in your chocolate brownie."

That would be a completely irresponsible attitude and a recipe for disaster, though exactly what we mean by worrying about it is a question that can be asked. Perhaps it is not worry to take sensible precautions and ask questions about the presence of nuts, lactose, gluten or whatever our allergy or intolerance is.

It could be that this is 'Jesus on menu planning'. Maybe he's saying, "There's no need to think about what you buy at the supermarket; there'll be something to feed the family for the next week one way or another because God knows you need to eat."

That's slightly less irresponsible but is still a very strange way to interpret the Bible. We've seen what Jesus said so let's look again and see if we can work out what he's on about. As I've said, it comes down to context again. The passage we looked at is not isolated; it starts with a joining word and one of our favourites for provoking a question.

"Therefore, I tell you, do not worry..."[23]

Therefore.

When you see that, always ask, "What's the 'therefore' there for?" It directs us back to at least the preceding verse or section. In this case the preceding verse says, *"No-one can serve two masters. Either you will hate the one and love the other, or you will be devoted to the one and despise the other. You cannot serve God and Money."*[24]

That helps a lot. It means that what Jesus is telling us is that the happy kind of attitude that he expresses in his advice about not worrying comes from an orientation of life that loves one master. Jesus is saying that a life devoted to serving God rather than Money and the material stuff of the world around us is the kind of life that does not need to worry.

---

[23] Matthew 6:25
[24] Matthew 6:24

It doesn't mean those who follow Jesus don't need food and drink or clothes. It doesn't mean we don't have to plant and sow and reap and harvest and store. What it does mean is that those necessary activities are not the 'be all and end all' of life. They are necessary to keep the body going but if they become the only point, we've lost the plot.

As always Jesus is talking on several levels. It is about our attitudes to food and drink and clothes. It is about sitting more lightly to decisions that sometimes take ages to make about exactly what to put on the table or which drink to order. And some people who seem to be naturally of an anxious disposition could do well to hear that message. It is even worth remembering that Paul underlines it when he says, *"Do not be anxious about anything, but in every situation, by prayer and petition, with thanksgiving, present your requests to God."*[25]

In other words, put God front and central in your outlook on life and the worries about other things fall into perspective.

But it is not just about our attitudes. Paul's words remind us of other words of Jesus in this passage. Jesus is talking as much about God in relation to us and God's knowledge of our needs as about us in our attitudes to material things.

'Look at the birds of the air; they don't sow or reap or store away in barns, and yet your heavenly Father feeds them.'[26]

The point is not that the birds have everything handed to them on a plate without needing to worry. Only yesterday I was watching a woodpecker foraging around on the grass digging up all kinds of tasty things to eat. That bird went out to get food. The point is that the birds don't worry about it. Often, I listen to birds singing away in the trees and know they are probably quite well fed. At that point they've visited the birdfeeder, dug up the worms and taken advantage of all the tasty snacks that my gardening has unearthed for them and they can sit and sing.

Jesus is drawing attention to the God who made all this: the God who delights in creativity and diversity, the God who wants joy and peace and harmony for all creation; the God who knows that there is

---

[25] Philippians 4:6
[26] Matthew 6:26

always enough to go round as long as we all have respect for one another and value the contribution and identity and life of all the other groups and individuals.

Jesus makes the same point with the beauty of the flowers. God is a God who makes the wonders and beauty of flowers and trees and fish in so many species, many of which are never seen by anyone and which are here today and gone tomorrow. Surely if we give God the glory and give God the attention and seek the ways of his Kingdom of love, joy, peace, beauty and harmony, then we will be OK. But we need to take some responsibility rather than assume God will work magic if we are irresponsible and don't ask about ingredients when we have nut allergy.

This is the point at which the Sermon on the Mount really can't quite do without chapter 6. The climax comes at the end of this passage. Focus on God's Kingdom and the ways of righteousness: living well with others in the ways of peace and justice, joy and harmony. When you aim at all of that, then the other things that we tend to worry about in food and drink and clothes will all fall into place in proper perspective.

8

Jesus on Water Quality

The Samaritan Woman at the Well

John 4:1-30

Now Jesus learned that the Pharisees had heard that he was gaining and baptising more disciples than John – although in fact it was not Jesus who baptised, but his disciples. So he left Judea and went back once more to Galilee. Now he had to go through Samaria. So he came to a town in Samaria called Sychar, near the plot of ground Jacob had given to his son Joseph. Jacob's well was there, and Jesus, tired as he was from the journey, sat down by the well. It was about noon.

When a Samaritan woman came to draw water, Jesus said to her, 'Will you give me a drink?' (His disciples had gone into the town to buy food.)

The Samaritan woman said to him, 'You are a Jew and I am a Samaritan woman. How can you ask me for a drink?' (For Jews do not associate with Samaritans.)

Jesus answered her, 'If you knew the gift of God and who it is that asks you for a drink, you would have asked him and he would have given you living water.'

'Sir,' the woman said, 'you have nothing to draw with and the well is deep. Where can you get this living water? Are you greater than our father Jacob, who gave us the well and drank from it himself, as did also his sons and his livestock?'

Jesus answered, 'Everyone who drinks this water will be thirsty again, but whoever drinks the water I give them will never thirst. Indeed, the water I give them will become in them a spring of water welling up to eternal life.'

The woman said to him, 'Sir, give me this water so that I won't get thirsty and have to keep coming here to draw water.'

He told her, 'Go, call your husband and come back.'

'I have no husband,' she replied.

Jesus said to her, 'You are right when you say you have no husband. The fact is, you have had five husbands, and the man you now have is not your husband. What you have just said is quite true.'

'Sir,' the woman said, 'I can see that you are a prophet. Our ancestors worshipped on this mountain, but you Jews claim that the place where we must worship is in Jerusalem.'

'Woman,' Jesus replied, 'believe me, a time is coming when you will worship the Father neither on this mountain nor in Jerusalem. You Samaritans worship what you do not know; we worship what we do know, for salvation is from the Jews. Yet a time is coming and has now come when the true worshippers will worship the Father in the Spirit and in truth, for they are the kind of worshippers the Father seeks. God is spirit, and his worshippers must worship in the Spirit and in truth.'

The woman said, 'I know that Messiah' (called Christ) 'is coming. When he comes, he will explain everything to us.'

Then Jesus declared, 'I, the one speaking to you – I am he.'

Just then his disciples returned and were surprised to find him talking with a woman. But no one asked, 'What do you want?' or 'Why are you talking with her?'

Then, leaving her water jar, the woman went back to the town and said to the people, 'Come, see a man who told me everything I've ever done. Could this be the Messiah?' They came out of the town and made their way towards him.

I've just been to refill the water tank that we have with our caravan. Obviously, when we're away with our caravan we don't have mains running water. We fill a forty-litre tank which stands outside the van and a pump enables us to get water from the taps in the kitchen and washroom areas. It's a job that has to be done at least every day – more often if either of us has had a shower. Sometimes when I fill up the tank I see others doing the same but usually people go at different times. It could be a much more social occasion than it is but no one times the need to fill up to coincide with others. It's a feature of modern life and outlook that we want these jobs to take as little time as possible.

I only have to do this when we're away caravanning, so I don't worry about it or wish it were not the case. At home we have mains running water. If I had to go to a stand pipe at least once every day and fill up a tank or a large jar, as many people in the world do, I might long for mains water to be laid on at home.

There's no discernible difference between the water that comes out of our water tank in the caravan and the water that comes out of the mains taps at home, but for many who do have to fetch water there is a difference. The difference is most likely to be noticeable when it has to be fetched from a source that is lying still – maybe even stagnant – like a pool or perhaps a well.

In biblical times there was a way in which they summed up the difference between water from a pool or a well and water from a stream that was flowing. The flowing water was called 'living water'.

Jesus' conversation about water with a woman by a well outside a town called Sychar in Samaria features this phrase. As usual with Jesus' conversations, especially those which John records, there are double meanings going on and several 'signpost' words and phrases.

There isn't space to explore all of them here so we'll concentrate on the water, but we'll need to notice some of the others as well.

The first, slightly oblique reference to water is that Jesus (or his disciples, at any rate) was baptising and getting a greater following than John the Baptist. Baptism involved being immersed in a river and stood for a change of life, the washing away of the old and a turning to the ways of God. It was and is a sign of renewal of life as God's people. It would not be untypical of John to introduce a section like this with a sideways reference to his subject matter in this way.

But John tells a story well and hides his points in the narrative. Jesus had to go through Samaria. Geographically that was the direct route but politically, and often with an eye to safety, many Jews of Jesus' day would go the long way round via Jericho in order to avoid Samaria. Going the direct route, they might come into contact with the less than 'pure' Samaritans or risk attack.

Perhaps Jesus' story about a man going from Jerusalem to Jericho where he fell among thieves and was helped not by one of his own people but by a Samaritan has more irony than we usually notice!

So Jesus didn't have to go through Samaria. He *chose* to go through Samaria unless this is *"had to"* in a vocational sense: he felt a compulsion. Maybe John is deliberately showing that Jesus was open to all possibilities for his message and therefore had to go through Samaria where there might be opportunities which wouldn't arise if he didn't. We know that on another occasion he took the longer route.

It is worth asking how often we do something similar. Do we intentionally go to places where we might have an opportunity to talk to someone about Jesus' message? Do we look for ways to make conversations happen that give us a chance to share something of our faith? Do we take a different route or shop in a different place or at a different time so that we might meet different people and strike up conversation? Jesus seems to have ignored many of the conventions and expectations of his time in order to bring his message to those who were marginalised by the mainstream religious establishment.

We see it as a natural occurrence that Jesus strikes up a conversation when someone else comes to the well. Most of us are not so introverted that we wouldn't acknowledge another person by the water tap at the caravan site. We need to pause to understand that for many reasons this conversation should never have happened. We've already seen that many Jews of Jesus' day would not have gone through Samaria in the first place. Any Jew with anything approaching Jesus' reputation would certainly not have been seen talking alone with a woman, for fear of gossip and accusations of immorality.

The other reason they should never have met is that it is the wrong time of day for her to be drawing water. To go out for water in the heat of the day means that she was avoiding the other women. Later in the account, we understand that was because of the reputation she already had for immorality, which Jesus appears to be able to see.

John points out that they were by *"Jacob's well"*. The story requires that we know there was a well, but John almost labours the connection with Jacob – one of the founding fathers of the nation of Israel. A little later in the conversation the woman makes a further reference to the fact that it is Jacob's well and its connection with him and his family and the life of their flocks and herds. That's the well this woman comes to draw water from. Later in the conversation she expresses some of the religious confusion there is between Jews and Samaritans, but basically, she is drawing on the traditions of Israel. That's where she gets the water that sustains her spirituality.

I hope that you're beginning to see the kind of double meaning for water that is going on in John's narrative. It is literal water – from the well – and there's also a spiritual sense to it.

Jesus sees an opportunity which he initiates by asking a question indicating that she could do something for him. When she expresses her surprise that he would even speak to her, he quickly raises the subject of a different kind of water. He offers her *"living water"*.

Not surprisingly, she doesn't understand his double meaning and simply wonders both how and where he's going to get water that is flowing. There is just a well; he has neither bucket nor stream.

As the conversation quickly develops, he has said enough to raise her interest and express her dissatisfaction with her present lifestyle. It almost sounds as though he's offered mains water to someone who has spent an hour or two of every day of their life walking to fetch water from a stagnant pool. That might be one of the ways of describing the transformation in someone's life when they see and accept what Jesus has to offer. How often, we might ask ourselves, do we realise that's what we can offer to those we meet and speak with day by day?

As the story progresses, we realise that John is cramming in more than a description of the life-changing offer that following Jesus presents. The character of the woman is well drawn and Jesus' approach is well described. He knows, as we should when we talk with people about following him, that it is not all about sitting at home drinking fresh, clear mains water via the cooler on the fridge. If the past is to be moved on from, it also has to be faced.

That is the point at which the conversation gets uncomfortable for her and she tries to distract him, as so many people do, by talking about religion and places of worship rather than the true spiritual nature of a relationship with God. Jesus is not distracted but tells her very politely but assertively that the question of places of worship is not relevant. Still she tries to wriggle out of the personal issues by suggesting that all these controversies and difficult questions will be settled when the Messiah comes and sorts it all out.

So far, all that Jesus has done in terms of starting a conversation, turning it to spiritual matters and refusing to be deflected from the personal nature of his offer, are things we can all do if we look for the opportunities. The next point that Jesus makes is one we shouldn't do. When she appealed to the coming of the Messiah in order to postpone the facing of personal issues, Jesus said, *"I, the one speaking to you – I am he."*[27]

Let's be quite plain. Don't claim to be the Messiah. We can't do that; it isn't true and it won't help.

What you can do is say that he has already come and that's what Jesus is all about and he does settle these distracting matters. If you can't think how, there's a good possibility you can find someone who has thought about them at the church you attend.

There's one more oblique reference to this woman's acceptance of Jesus' offer of *"living water"* rather than the sort she was in the habit of drawing from Jacob's well. Jesus' disciples returned and broke up

---

[27] John 4:26

the conversation. It seems he had done enough because she went back and told her neighbours about him. The interesting phrase from the point of view of her acceptance of Jesus' offer of *"living water"* is that she left her water jar behind.

It's as though she knew she didn't need it anymore – in the spiritual sense that she had access to the living water that wells up from within to eternal life. John returns to this theme in chapter 7 again in the context of debate about who Jesus is. He describes Jesus' announcement of rivers of living water flowing from within those who follow him and explains what we have been wondering since reading about the living water offered to the woman by Jacob's well.

By this he meant the Spirit, whom those who believed in him were later to receive.[28]

9

Jesus on Sourcing Lunch

Food You Know Nothing About

John 4:27-38

Just then his disciples returned and were surprised to find him talking with a woman. But no one asked, 'What do you want?' or 'Why are you talking with her?'

Then, leaving her water jar, the woman went back to the town and said to the people, 'Come, see a man who told me everything I've ever done. Could this be the Messiah?' They came out of the town and made their way towards him.

Meanwhile his disciples urged him, 'Rabbi, eat something.'

But he said to them, 'I have food to eat that you know nothing about.'

Then his disciples said to each other, 'Could someone have brought him food?'

'My food,' said Jesus, 'is to do the will of him who sent me and to finish his work. Don't you have a saying, "It's still four months until harvest"? I tell you, open your eyes and look at the fields! They are ripe for harvest. Even now the one who

reaps draws a wage and harvests a crop for eternal life, so that the sower and the reaper may be glad together. Thus the saying "One sows and another reaps" is true. I sent you to reap what you have not worked for. Others have done the hard work, and you have reaped the benefits of their labour.'

No doubt you can identify with the feeling that an activity you've been engaged in has been draining. You find it harder to concentrate and feel tired and hungry afterwards. If you've had a break, you find it difficult to summon the energy to return to the task.

I wonder if you can also identify with the opposite? There's something that you do which really excites you, you can't wait to get back to it after a break or you forget to stop. This would be the subject we're talking about if we meet for a coffee and half an hour later yours is untouched and going cold because you've been telling me about _____. When you finish that activity, you are buzzing with energy and it's as though you've had several sugary drinks. The last thing on your mind is having something to eat.

As soon as you start to look for them, you find double meanings all over John's Gospel. At the beginning of John's account of Jesus' conversation with the woman at Jacob's well outside Sychar in Samaria, he tells us that Jesus' disciples went into town to buy food. It's the middle of the day so this is a lunch stop. John also tells us that Jesus is tired when he sits by the well.

They come back just after Jesus has got to the key part of his conversation. He is talking about living water and his role as Messiah – saviour – who comes and makes the awkward and distracting questions irrelevant. When the woman leaves them, they remember that Jesus had been tired and hungry so they urge him to have something to eat.

So far, it's a natural course of events: disciples return, woman leaves, they urge him to have some of the food they've bought.

But he said to them, 'I have food to eat that you know nothing about.'[29]

Not surprisingly, they wonder if someone's brought him something. Perhaps the woman he was talking to knew of a café or a local

---

[29] John 4:32

supermarket that sold sandwiches just round the corner that they didn't find. Maybe she had some lunch with her to eat while she fetched her water and she shared it with him. Surely, they might even wonder, he didn't bring some rolls out from breakfast at their B&B without telling them?

All are possible questions to go through their heads because they don't yet understand Jesus' double meanings.

Jesus is referring to the feeling you get when you've been doing what you were meant for. He explains that he's been doing God's work; what he has been engaged in has been completely in line with what God wants; he doesn't need food – he's buzzing with energy from activity that fulfils his vocation.

Hopefully that explains something of what happened and a response that sounds a little odd. But it only helps us understand a little better a passage from the Bible. That's one stage of working out what it's all about but the second essential stage is to work out what it is *still* all about – what it's all about for *us*, now; not just what it was all about then.

Just hearing that *"to do the will of him who sent me and to finish his work"*[30] is like having lunch for Jesus might make us wonder what it is that works like that for us. Well, we can find out. What is it that you were talking about while your coffee went cold? What is it that you do that gives you energy rather than makes you tired? What is it that you do in your Christian life that seems to take on a new dimension, go so unexpectedly smoothly or have results beyond those of others?

Answering those questions gets you some way towards finding your 'food that others know nothing about'.

We might also be encouraged to explore these questions by the enthusiasm that Jesus shares with his disciples. This is the kind of excitement that doing God's work can give us.

Jesus talks about sowing and reaping and how the usual gap in between has been narrowed so that the sower and reaper are glad together. This is not about the discovery of a miracle crop that comes to fruition as soon as it's sown. This is about Jesus' excitement at discovering an opportunity for sharing about God's work and his

---

[30] John 4:34

presence where people are ready to hear and respond as soon as the subject is mentioned.

This is what happens when people discover their God-given gifts and exercise them in accordance with his will. This is what happens when we are on the lookout for opportunities and know how to use them. When we go looking for the work of God in a place or among a community, we find that he is already there.

Jesus used a story to illustrate this, which was about how the time between sowing and reaping is not necessarily long, and the importance of being observant to spot the signs when there is a harvest to be gathered in. There's a story told at the end of the Church Army Faith Pictures Course which is worth repeating as a different illustration.

Some rangers were transporting a leopard from one reserve to another in South Africa but the van they were in was involved in an incident in the suburbs of Johannesburg and the leopard escaped. Realising they could be in very serious trouble if the leopard mauled someone or even killed someone, they called for help and armed rangers searched the streets of the suburbs looking for the leopard. On the first evening they looked, they found six leopards – at least five of which they didn't know were there.

If you're looking for opportunities to exercise your gifts; if you're looking for opportunities to share your faith; if you're looking for opportunities to do the will of the one who calls and sends you and finish his work, you may well find that he's been there before you and you'll find more leopards in the suburbs of Johannesburg than you thought were there.

There could be a café just round the corner that others know nothing about.

10

Jesus on Hospitality (i)

The House of Simon the Pharisee

Luke 7:36-50

When one of the Pharisees invited Jesus to have dinner with him, he went to the Pharisee's house and reclined at the table. A woman in that town who lived a sinful life learned that Jesus was eating at the Pharisee's house, so she came there with an alabaster jar of perfume. As she stood behind him at his feet weeping, she began to wet his feet with her tears. Then she wiped them with her hair, kissed them and poured perfume on them.

When the Pharisee who had invited him saw this, he said to himself, 'If this man were a prophet, he would know who is touching him and what kind of woman she is – that she is a sinner.'

Jesus answered him, 'Simon, I have something to tell you.'

'Tell me, teacher,' he said.

'Two people owed money to a certain money-lender. One owed him five hundred denarii, and the other fifty. Neither of

them had the money to pay him back, so he forgave the debts of both. Now which of them will love him more?'

Simon replied, 'I suppose the one who had the bigger debt forgiven.'

'You have judged correctly,' Jesus said.

Then he turned towards the woman and said to Simon, 'Do you see this woman? I came into your house. You did not give me any water for my feet, but she wet my feet with her tears and wiped them with her hair. You did not give me a kiss, but this woman, from the time I entered, has not stopped kissing my feet. You did not put oil on my head, but she has poured perfume on my feet. Therefore, I tell you, her many sins have been forgiven – as her great love has shown. But whoever has been forgiven little loves little.' Then Jesus said to her, 'Your sins are forgiven.'

The other guests began to say among themselves, 'Who is this who even forgives sins?'

Jesus said to the woman, 'Your faith has saved you; go in peace.'

How do you treat guests when they come to dinner?

- Do you take their coats and hang them in the hall or leave them to take them off as they make their way through and perhaps leave them on the banister?
- Do you indicate the cloakroom and give them the opportunity to wash and make themselves comfortable before you take them into the dining room?
- Do you shake their hand or offer a hug, or do you wave them straight on up the hall and hardly even make eye contact?
- Do you ask after their journey and offer them a drink, or do you take them straight to the table where the food is already waiting?
- Do you check beforehand about any dietary requirements and give them a tablespoon to help themselves to vegetables, or do you sit them down and put a plate of food in front of them?

Any or all of these may or may not be part of your culture's etiquette of hospitality, but the point is that most cultures have some etiquette of hospitality. In Jesus' culture the equivalent of the cloakroom was some water to wash your feet; the equivalent of a handshake or hug was a kiss on the cheek; the equivalent of offering a drink was to pour oil on the head of an honoured guest. Many of these may seem strange to those living in twenty-first century British culture but they were what was expected in Jesus' situation.

Another key question about hospitality is whether you treat all your guests the same. It may be that some of the closest family don't get treated as guests at all while others may be given special treatment because you want to impress for some reason. Or maybe the way you treat guests depends on how you see them in relation to yourself.

- Have they come because you hope they might be a useful contact?
- Have they come because you want to check out their reputation and you're almost giving them an interview?
- Have they come because they're friends and you visit them sometimes?
- Have they come because you feel you want to repay them for a kindness they've shown?

It seems that Jesus was invited to dinner with Simon the Pharisee because Simon wanted to check out Jesus' reputation as a prophet. That puts him on the more open end of the spectrum as regards Pharisees' responses to Jesus but it's not a comfortable situation. We could speculate about the conversation as Simon proceeded to interview Jesus, but Luke tells us nothing about it.

Another question about hospitality might be about how open your home is. Do you keep the door shut and only allow in people you invite, or do you leave the door open so that anyone can come in and watch your dinner parties? I suspect your dinner parties are fairly private affairs unless you're in the habit of streaming them live on social media.

That's another aspect of our culture that is very different from Jesus' time and place. Their houses were very open places where almost anyone could come in and out. Some dinner parties would have been almost spectator sports as people gathered around a courtyard watching guests and seeing who went to eat with whom.

While Jesus is eating at Simon's house an unnamed woman from the town comes in. Luke tells us just enough of her background for us to know that this is a significant encounter. Luke tells us the one about 'Jesus, the Pharisee and the sinful woman'.

Another hospitality issue is how well you know your guests. Or for that matter, when you visit how well do you know your hosts? Do you know what sort of people they are – really?

Simon sees his opportunity to catch Jesus out and prove that he's not really a prophet. If he were a prophet, he would know what kind of woman she is.[31]

The thing is, he *does* know. Jesus knows what she has been and he also knows what she is. He knows she has led a sinful life. But he knows that she is forgiven because she weeps in his presence even before she opens her jar of perfume. As if that were not bad enough, she makes matters worse by letting her hair down in public so she can wipe his feet dry from the tears. No respectable woman would do that in company – it's almost equivalent to taking her clothes off. And then she does as she always intended and anoints his feet with the perfume demonstrating just how much she knows herself forgiven and loved by the God she sees made real before her in Jesus.

Jesus not only knows what kind of woman she has been and what kind of woman she has become; he also turns the tables on Simon because he knows what he's thinking. It is a potentially awkward situation but Jesus is never phased by being put on the spot. He always has a story as a gentle way to stick the knife in.

It seems that Simon's hospitality is at least generous enough to allow his guest time to tell a story and Jesus tells the one about the money-lender and the debtors. It's an unusual story because the money-lender isn't calling in the bailiffs but seems to have sufficient resources to write off large debts. Five hundred denarii is approaching eighteen months' wages for a day labourer – maybe about £30,000 in today's money. Fifty denarii (£3,000) is also not a small amount but both debts have been forgiven. It is not hard to work out which debtor is more grateful. In terms of hospitality, the

---

one forgiven more is likely to lay on the most lavish party to say thank you.

Simon is bright enough to see the answer. Luke doesn't tell us his reaction when Jesus points out what the story is about in terms of what has just happened in Simon's dining room.

Once again Jesus has used an occasion where food is involved to make a point about something else. This event is only incidentally about hospitality though some of the points it raises are important ones to consider.

What Jesus is pointing out is that our behaviour and our reactions in his presence are not questions and issues to be explored as we test out who he really is. What Jesus wants us to see is that his coming is the expression of a God of love who offers forgiveness for the largest and smallest of debts. The person with the reputation for a sinful life and the person whose sins are kept secret are both forgiven as they come to him knowing that all they owe is devotion.

11

Jesus on Bread (i)

I am the Bread of Life

John 6:47-59

'Very truly I tell you, the one who believes has eternal life. I am the bread of life. Your ancestors ate the manna in the wilderness, yet they died. But here is the bread that comes down from heaven, which anyone may eat and not die. I am the living bread that came down from heaven. Whoever eats this bread will live for ever. This bread is my flesh, which I will give for the life of the world.'

Then the Jews began to argue sharply among themselves, 'How can this man give us his flesh to eat?'

Jesus said to them, 'Very truly I tell you, unless you eat the flesh of the Son of Man and drink his blood, you have no life in you. Whoever eats my flesh and drinks my blood has eternal life, and I will raise them up at the last day. For my flesh is real food and my blood is real drink. Whoever eats my flesh and drinks my blood remains in me, and I in them. Just as the living Father sent me and I live because of the Father, so the one who feeds on me will live because of me. This is the bread that came down from heaven. Your ancestors ate manna and died, but whoever feeds on this bread will live for ever.' He said this while teaching in the synagogue in Capernaum.

If Jesus is talking about food, we might very reasonably suppose that he has completely lost the plot here.

No one – much less a Jew – talks about people eating his own flesh and drinking his own blood. Maybe we echo Jesus' disciples when they said, *"This is a hard teaching."*[32]

It brings us to a key tool in reading John's Gospel in particular. Right at the beginning John has given us the tool when he said, *"The Word became flesh."*[33] This principle in John's thinking works its way through the whole creation and gives us sacramental thinking. The spiritual becomes solid and material in order that we might know it for what it is.

So, the word became flesh. We do not live on bread alone but on every word that comes from God. Jesus calls himself the bread of life. He gives us himself to sustain us for eternal life just as we are sustained during the day by eating bread. But it is not enough simply to think of Jesus and remember that we're sustained. Because life is bodily and material, it has to have a bodily and material way of being known.

The words John uses to write this make it very clear that he is not thinking of a purely spiritual, meditative event with grateful contemplation for all that Jesus was and did and said. He could have simply used words like 'eat' and 'feed', but the word he used has a much more physical sense to it. It might be better translated 'munch' or 'chew'.

John wants us to know that Jesus thought we should actually eat and drink, and not simply engage in a spiritual exercise of the mind.

So perhaps Jesus is talking about food and drink after all. He's talking about the way we use them to get at something much deeper.

As we get used to interpreting Jesus' words and John's ways of reporting them, we start to understand that there must be some reference going on that perhaps we've missed but might have been

---

[32] John 6:60
[33] John 1:14

more apparent to the original readers. Often, when we find that reference it starts to make more sense.

So, where else might we find anything about eating someone's flesh or drinking someone's blood?

Jesus' reference to drinking his blood comes as a bit of a surprise. We might just have got used to the idea that he is the *"bread of life"* and that in some way we are to eat his flesh to partake of this bread. But, we might ask, where did drinking his blood come from?

A further thought on the subject reinforces the need to ask the question. The whole point of kosher preparation of meat is that the blood is drained out so there is no danger of eating or drinking it. How can Jews talk about drinking blood?

When we find the reference, it starts to make more sense.

In 2 Samuel 23 and 1 Chronicles 11 we read of a time when the Philistines had occupied King David's home town of Bethlehem. David and his army were in a tight place and David expressed out loud how much he longed for a drink from the well in Bethlehem. Three of his bravest and most loyal fighting men heard him, broke through the Philistine lines, got water from the well at Bethlehem and brought it back to David.

But David didn't drink it. He said that to do so would be like drinking their blood because they had risked their lives for it and for him. No Jew would think of drinking blood as it was absolutely forbidden under the law. That's why David made the comparison. It is also why Jesus talked about drinking his blood in the same breath as eating his flesh.

Just as David refused to benefit from the risk to their lives that his fighting men had taken, so Jesus is saying that to benefit from what he is doing, God's people who are part of the new Exodus (pointed to by the feeding with the loaves) must eat his flesh and drink his blood.

The benefit from what he is doing is that they will be raised up on the last day and live for ever.

Clearly, when Jesus said, *"I am the bread of life ... the living bread that came down from heaven ... Whoever eats my flesh and drinks my blood has eternal life, and I will raise them up at the last day,"*[34] he was not talking about cannibalism.

---

[34] John 6:48,51,54

But he is talking about real food and real drink and not just a spiritualised thought process. In his account of the last supper John does not record any actual eating or drinking and he doesn't record Jesus' words at the supper about bread and wine and the instruction to break bread and share wine to remember him.[35] Instead, this is where John chooses to place his sacramental ideas about Jesus' body and blood.

In the light of the story about David and the water from Bethlehem, we can see that Jesus will go further than David's three brave heroes. Jesus, as the Messiah who comes to save the world, will not only put his life at risk but he will actually lose his life. His comrades then and all his followers since will benefit from his death. They, and we, will have their thirst for the real and eternal presence of God quenched by his death. We drink his blood and eat his flesh.

The manna in the wilderness in Exodus, which the feeding of the five thousand obviously referred to, was a practical sign of God's care in sustaining his people. Jesus is saying that he is much more than that. The word became flesh so that God's presence might be made real for us. In a similar way Jesus gave us bread and wine so that the way he feeds and sustains us for eternal life might also be made real for us.

---

[35] We'll look at that in chapter 20

12

Jesus on the Cooking Rota

Martha and Mary

Luke 10:38-42

As Jesus and his disciples were on their way, he came to a village where a woman named Martha opened her home to him. She had a sister called Mary, who sat at the Lord's feet listening to what he said. But Martha was distracted by all the preparations that had to be made. She came to him and asked, 'Lord, don't you care that my sister has left me to do the work by myself? Tell her to help me!'

'Martha, Martha,' the Lord answered, 'you are worried and upset about many things, but few things are needed – or indeed only one. Mary has chosen what is better, and it will not be taken away from her.'

It's not so long since our daughters were at university, and when we visited their student houses, I sometimes noticed rotas stuck on walls, doors or the fridge to indicate whose turn it was for some of the household jobs. This was usually about cleaning rather than cooking because students tend to eat separately from others in their households as they have very different schedules from one another. But in some other households the chores may be divided out fairly, including a person designated to cook on any particular day. In other households the various chores tend to fall to the same person almost all the time. The washing may be done by one person, the cleaning by another and the cooking by another depending on who is likely to be most available at the time. In our house, when there are guests or a special occasion, everybody helps out to make sure the house is clean and tidy and there's a suitable meal prepared.

When we look at this story, often known as the story of Mary and Martha, and ask ourselves the usual question, "What's that all about, then?" there are a number of possible answers which are at best only part of the answer.

It might be about the cooking rota.

Perhaps Martha is cross that Jesus turned up the day she was down to cook. Mary may have cooked the previous day for the two or three of them. Luke doesn't mention Lazarus, the sisters' brother[36]. This is not about Jesus telling people to stick to the rota.

An important tool for interpretation is context and it is interesting that Luke places this story too early in his narrative. Jesus has just 'resolutely set out for Jerusalem'[37] and will not go through Jericho until chapter 19. Martha and Mary lived in Bethany at the Jerusalem end of the Jericho Road, near the city where people came from to mourn with them when their brother died. It looks as though Luke has placed it at this point in his narrative so that it immediately follows the parable of the Good Samaritan.

There the Samaritan was commended for his activity in caring for a person in need. In this story there is another aspect of discipleship to be commended. Luke makes it clear that Martha is the main character.

- It is Martha who opened her home to Jesus.
- It is Martha who is distracted by the practical preparations that have to be made.
- It is Martha who comes to Jesus to complain that she is doing all the work.

Usually we read from Jesus' reply to Martha that she shouldn't worry about it and Mary is doing the right thing.

---

[36] John 11 and 12
[37] Luke 9:51

It looks like a rebuke to Martha, almost as though Jesus is telling her to leave the cooking and come and sit down and listen. This all hangs on the phrase about *"few things"* or *"only one"* thing being necessary. The commentators tell us that the source for this is very uncertain and may be a very early piece of interpretation that has crept into the narrative.

It should not for that reason be ignored. It serves to emphasise the point that listening to Jesus and learning from him is of great importance. In placing this account just after the parable of the Good Samaritan where action is commended, Luke reminds us that action is not everything – we are to listen and learn as well.

Part of what this story is about is the balance between activity and learning, between serving our neighbours and listening to God.

But that's not all of what this is about. Luke draws the scene vividly with Martha making preparations and Mary sitting listening to Jesus in another part of the house: Martha *"came to him..."*[38] It is often in the little phrases that draw the scene that we find clues to what it is all about. In this case it tells us about the areas of the house. There is the area for preparation of food and there is separately an area where guests sit and talk. In first century Jewish houses these areas would have been fairly strictly demarcated on gender lines. The women's area was in the kitchen; the men's area was what we would call the living room. The sexes mixed only outside with the children or in a married couple's bedroom.

An important part of what this is about is crossing boundaries. Jesus is doing it all the time when he goes into Samaritan areas and Gentile areas, and Luke has made sure he emphasised this movement in his narrative. But it is not only geographical boundaries that Jesus crosses. Luke also shows that Jesus crosses the cultural and sociological boundaries as well. Jesus mixes with Samaritans and Gentiles and teaches and heals in their areas. In this story Jesus crosses domestic boundaries – or at least encourages others to do so. The role of listening and learning is not just for the men.

There's another little descriptive phrase that Luke uses to emphasise the crossing of this boundary. Mary "sat at the Lord's feet listening to what he said". Much of the art depicting this scene has

---

[38] Luke 10:40

taken the phrase literally and places Mary sitting on the floor looking up adoringly into Jesus' face as he teaches. This is to sentimentalise and misunderstand.

It sentimentalises because it reads in a romantic attachment on the part of Mary, and possibly also Martha, which is not in the text in any sense. It misunderstands because it takes *"sitting at his feet"* literally. To sit at the feet of the rabbi was to learn from the teacher: to be a disciple, to be one who was training to do as he did. Elsewhere we read that Paul *"sat at the feet of Gamaliel"[39]*. It doesn't mean that he sat on the floor gazing adoringly up into the face of the rabbi. It means Gamaliel was his teacher, the rabbi from whom he learned his trade much as an apprentice learns a trade from a master craftsman.

So this is justification for women being included as much as men in listening and learning from Jesus but that's not enough. Given the context of this story just after the parable of the Good Samaritan, it is not simply to tell us that listening to the word of God is better than serving his people.

Another strand to the story is that of the different temperaments which combine to make a diverse humanity. Activists will resonate with Martha; contemplatives will resonate with Mary, in the roles which Luke describes. Similarly, people who are task-focussed will identify with the role Martha took while those who focus on people will identify with Mary. It is not Jesus' purpose to make people from either end of the spectrum feel that they should be on the other end.

When we read Jesus' answer to Martha as meaning she has chosen the wrong role, we misinterpret him and read in more than Luke intended. It is clear that food has to be prepared and someone has to do that. Activists will always be quicker to get started on those tasks. What Jesus is telling us is that although tasks have to be done, if we are to be his disciples the one thing that is necessary as a basis for all that activity is to stop and listen to his word as he teaches. Make sure that everyone gets some time off the cooking rota so they can listen and learn.

---

[39] Acts 22:3

13

Jesus on Hospitality (ii)

The Friend at Midnight

Luke 11:5-8

Then Jesus said to them, 'Suppose you have a friend, and you go to him at midnight and say, "Friend, lend me three loaves of bread; a friend of mine on a journey has come to me, and I have no food to offer him." And suppose the one inside answers, "Don't bother me. The door is already locked, and my children and I are in bed. I can't get up and give you anything." I tell you, even though he will not get up and give you the bread because of friendship, yet because of your shameless audacity he will surely get up and give you as much as you need.'

It is late at night; you've made the shopping list for the morning, when you will get food in to last the next week, but for now there's nothing in the fridge or the cupboard; you've put the lights out, locked the door and the whole household is asleep in bed.

There's an insistent knock at the door.

What do you do?

- Some would try to ignore it, turn over, put the pillow over their ears and try to go back to sleep.

- Some would peer out through an upstairs window to see who was making such a noise.
- Some would shout from their window that whoever was waking the neighbourhood should have more consideration and just go away.
- Some might wonder what emergency would prompt someone to knock on a door in the middle of the night; they might think it could be someone running away from attack or abuse.

Whichever of those options you choose, or if you choose a different response, suppose the person knocking so insistently at your door late at night turns out to be a friend on a journey who has been held up in traffic because of an accident on the motorway and their phone is out of charge. When they finally got off the motorway you were the nearest person they knew and what they need is a meal, a bed for the night and a place to charge their phone.

What do you do?

A bed is not too much of a problem once you get out the spare sheets and move any accumulated stuff off the spare bed. A place to charge the phone is easy. But food is more difficult. It is late and even the convenience stores are closed. Your local supermarkets all closed at midnight or before. You have nothing in the fridge or the cupboard, and you've already done the list for the weekly shop the next day.

Under such circumstances most of us would probably give our friend a bed and a place to charge the phone and apologise that there was no food. We would probably also feel it was a bit late to be making a meal anyway and make up our minds to be more organised about shopping in future so that there was always more than enough bread for breakfast. In most people's opinion that would all be going beyond the call of duty.

Jesus takes it for granted that what you do if a friend turns up unannounced late at night and you have no food in the house is go round to another friend and ask to borrow some bread.

In making that assumption he teaches us that we have much to learn from the rules and conventions of hospitality in his culture in the ancient Middle East. Jesus teaches us that friendship and hospitality are important aspects of culture and that we are not as generous as we think. We tend to think of ourselves and what is convenient and if we put ourselves out a bit, others should be grateful. In Jesus' culture the friend who limited his hospitality to what was possible and convenient only from his own inadequate resources would have felt disgraced.

Food, Jesus teaches us, is an essential element in hospitality and in friendship. We know it ourselves to some extent when it is automatic to offer cake or at least biscuits with the coffee when a friend calls.

But this must be about more than a lesson in the etiquette of hospitality even if it is taking the hypothetical situation to an extreme.

As always, the clue to what Jesus is talking about behind his advice about etiquette is in the context.

These verses follow after Luke's version of the Lord's Prayer when Jesus' disciples had asked him to teach them to pray. He goes on to talk about persistence in asking, seeking and knocking and likens God to a father who knows not to play bad jokes on his children. It is obvious that what Jesus is talking about behind this parable of cultural hospitality advice is prayer.

Firstly, this teaches us something about the God to whom we pray. He's like a friend who understands. The friend outside would do the same for the one in the house if the roles were reversed because he knows the hospitality rules. So with God, he understands us, he knows the situations we find ourselves in.

It also has to be said that there are several characteristics of God that this story doesn't teach us. God is not like a sleepy friend who reluctantly responds in spite of the inconvenience to himself and his family.

But the main point that Jesus teaches from this parable about prayer is persistence – a holy boldness that keeps asking, won't give up looking and is insistent in its knocking.

This is more than the routine of prayer that should be part of our daily and weekly pattern. There are too many things to pray about to have energy and insistence for all of them. It is good and right to have a regular time and pattern for prayer. For some that is the only way to make it happen at all. But it is unrealistic to think that we will pray for everything in some way at some time and that should cover it. There will be some subjects that are particularly close to our hearts on every level.

There will be personal issues relating to our own situation or the health and welfare of our families or the decisions our families, friends and colleagues are facing. There will also be local issues or questions about activities or personnel for certain roles in our local church or other organisation to which we belong. There will also be big national and international issues of peace, justice and reconciliation that keep cropping up in the same places and in different places.

Jesus' advice about prayer when he was asked to teach his disciples to pray was to be persistent.

- Don't stop asking for world leaders to have an attitude that looks for peace and reconciliation rather than provocation and revenge.
- Don't stop asking for attitudes of openness and hospitality among your church.
- Don't stop asking God to show you ways to serve your neighbours for the good of the whole community.
- Don't stop knocking at God's door when you want your colleagues to see something of his ways and run the business or organisation for the common good with as much grace and generosity as possible.

The inevitable question is, "Why does God need us to ask? Why doesn't he just give us what is right and good just because he knows that we need it?"

In a sense it is to misunderstand prayer if we ask the question. It is fair enough if prayer is about telling God something he doesn't know or persuading him round to our point of view. But the point of prayer is not that. As Jesus says in an only slightly different context, *"Your heavenly Father knows that you need them."*[40]

Prayer can be a risky activity because it changes the one who prays in two possible ways. One is that we may be required to be part of the answer to our prayers. If we pray for peace and reconciliation, we have to be prepared to be people of peace and reconciliation in our own relationships.

---

[40] Matthew 6:32; see also chapter 7

The other way in which prayer changes the one who prays is that it forms us and shapes what we think. So, if we persistently pray for change among oppressive regimes so there will be justice for the oppressed and freedom for those who are forced to flee, we will eventually develop a greater attitude of compassion for refugees. The attitudes move from being theoretical, academic attitudes about what we know to be right to become a part of our nature running through our veins and we become truly people of peace.

If we persistently ask God that his ways would be known on earth and among our communities; and if we persistently look for evidence of his Kingdom in our own circles of acquaintance; and if we persistently knock on his door for the basics of life for all his children, then we will receive the Holy Spirit, we will find that God is at work in our lives and our communities, the door will be opened for us to sit at table in his Kingdom.

As we are persistently bold in our prayers, we will be people of patience; we will not leap to hasty conclusions; we will act out of kindness and generosity; others will be able to count on us to follow through with what we say and be loyal to them; we will develop an outward appearance and an inner attitude of contentment and delight in all things good and beautiful; the ways in which we deal with people will not be harsh but will resolve disputes and calm people's fears and their anger.

In short, we will be people who love as God loves, we will have been changed, we will have been given the Holy Spirit to live in and through us because that is what we will have been asking for.

14

Jesus on Bread (ii)

The Parable of the Yeast

Luke 13:20-21

Again [Jesus] asked, 'What shall I compare the kingdom of God to? It is like yeast that a woman took and mixed into about thirty kilograms of flour until it worked all through the dough.'

As far as recipes go, this one is pretty minimal. It's a technical challenge that reads:

1. Take thirty kilogrammes of flour.
2. Make bread.

If Jesus is giving baking advice, it's not really enough. As usual, there's more to it. Also as usual, the clue is in the text and the context.

Jesus seldom opened his mouth without talking about the Kingdom of God. That's what he talked about and what he wanted people to know about. It also explains many of his actions because he wanted people to see what life is like when God is King; what life should be like; what life can be like if we allow God to be King.

Sometimes people get the wrong idea about what God being King means and they think it's a time that is probably a long way off. Sometimes the wrong idea they get is that God's Kingdom is only relevant when we think about heaven.

The other attitude people have with regard to the Kingdom of God is that they look around and see very little evidence of it so they get disheartened and wonder if there's any point to it at all.

This parable, along with the preceding one about the mustard seed[41], is meant to be encouraging. In some ways the message is the same. In the horticultural terms of the mustard seed parable, 'from tiny acorns grow mighty oaks'. A small thing can make a big difference and the Kingdom of God is like that. Put a small seed of the Kingdom in a community and watch great things grow from it to the benefit of many.

But that is to get stuck on the previous parable. There are very few occasions when Jesus told more than one story in succession with exactly the same point. Different analogies permit the appreciation of different aspects of the same view.

So a question about these two parables might be, "How is yeast in bread different from a seed growing into a tree?"

Well, both are organic processes but the growth of a seed is about the growth of something large out of something small. The rising of bread dough due to the action of yeast is about the effect on something large of something relatively small but powerful.

That's the encouragement. Look at whatever Kingdom activity you do or happens through your church. It may seem very small. Your food bank seems a very small contribution to the needs of so many people on low incomes or suffering from benefit sanctions. Your stand for fair treatment of a colleague at work might seem a tiny contribution to the need for justice in the world. The fact that you stopped and held the hand of the person knocked off her bike by a motorist driving too fast and too close while the ambulance came might not seem much when there is so much pain and hurt in the world. The fact that you sent a few pounds to a relief charity when you heard about an earthquake might seem a very small contribution when there is so much need.

---

[41] Luke 13:18-19; addressed in *Jesus on Gardening*, Onwards and Upwards 2017, chapter 8

But we need to be encouraged that all the tiny actions for justice, mercy and compassion are part of the establishment of the ways of God's Kingdom. As people see these small actions, they see the better way; they see that compassion and peace, justice and mercy rather than revenge and hatred are the ways to build a better world.

But, some will ask, what does that have to do with God's Kingdom? Surely we just have to wait for Jesus to return and establish that and in the meantime we just have to grin and bear it and get on as best we can?

Emphatically, *no!*

God's Kingdom is not about waiting for some time in the far future that it seems will never come. Jesus' central teaching about the Kingdom of God comes in the way he taught us to pray for it: *"Your Kingdom come ... on earth as in heaven."*[42]

The way God reigns is through actions of grace, mercy, justice, peace and compassion. Work that through the dough of this world by our actions and it rises like bread until God's reign is established – on earth as in heaven.

---

[42] Matthew 6:10, emphasis added

15

Jesus on the Seating Plan

Those Who Exalt Themselves Will Be Humbled

Luke 14:1-11

One Sabbath, when Jesus went to eat in the house of a prominent Pharisee, he was being carefully watched. There in front of him was a man suffering from abnormal swelling of his body. Jesus asked the Pharisees and experts in the law, 'Is it lawful to heal on the Sabbath or not?' But they remained silent. So taking hold of the man, he healed him and sent him on his way.

Then he asked them, 'If one of you has a child or an ox that falls into a well on the Sabbath day, will you not immediately pull it out?' And they had nothing to say.

When he noticed how the guests picked the places of honour at the table, he told them this parable: 'When someone invites you to a wedding feast, do not take the place of honour, for a person more distinguished than you may have been invited. If so, the host who invited both of you will come and say to you, "Give this person your seat." Then, humiliated, you will have to take the least important place. But when you are invited, take the lowest place, so that when your host comes, he will say to you, "Friend, move up to a better place." Then you will be honoured in the presence of all the other guests. For all those who exalt themselves will be humbled, and those who humble themselves will be exalted.'

At first sight this is a simple piece of social advice that is immediately transferable to a more modern setting. If this is a dinner party or drinks occasion and you want to make sure you network with the most important people, don't be too pushy or they might make their excuses and go and talk to someone else who is more important to them. Hang back a bit and be realistic about who you are and what you have to offer. The movers and shakers who make things happen will notice what you have to offer and invite you to share your experience and expertise.

In the dinner party setting, choose a place away from the host and you may be invited to come nearer, but choose a place near the host and you may find that there's someone they'd rather talk to and your embarrassment will be so public you may find no one wants to talk to you all evening.

The verses about places of honour sound more like a piece of practical wisdom than a story but Jesus doesn't give practical wisdom for its own sake. Luke gives us a clue that there is more to it by introducing the advice as a parable. There must be at least a second meaning below the surface.

As always, there is a clue in the context. The way Luke constructs his account of the occasion shows us what Jesus is talking about below the surface of his practical advice for social occasions.

Luke places several important episodes in Jesus' ministry in the context of a meal. Here he has been invited to eat with a prominent Pharisee. It is not the first time we've read about such an occasion. In chapter 7 Luke told us about a visit to Simon the Pharisee and hid a message about God's grace and generous welcome under a piece of advice about greeting guests.[43] Here the situation is similar, and Luke tells us that it is a Sabbath and Jesus was being carefully watched.

The man came in who had dropsy. Some translations simply say an abnormal swelling. It is swelling often in hands and feet caused by fluid retention that might in turn have been caused by a heart

---

[43] See chapter 10, Jesus on Hospitality (i)

condition. Luke tells us that Jesus was being closely watched so it is possible that the Pharisees and experts in the Law had manipulated the situation to try to catch him out. Equally, he may simply have come in, perhaps seeking Jesus as the woman at Simon's house had done.

Jesus is aware of the situation and takes control. Jesus asked about Sabbath observance, *"Is it lawful to heal on the Sabbath or not?"* They were unable to answer because if they said it was lawful, they could be accused of being lax in their attitude to the Law. If they said it wasn't lawful, they would be accused of a lack of compassion towards someone who was suffering. If Jesus had not asked the question, they would surely have criticised him for a lax attitude to the Law, but by remaining silent when he asked, they lost the right to criticise.

Jesus' second question about rescuing a child or an ox from a well on the Sabbath is related to the healing and is the kind of academic question that Pharisaic ethicists would often debate. Jesus makes sure that it is not just about a point of law but also a question of conscience. In academic circumstances they could debate about the ox and legitimately come to different conclusions but the man whose ox it was would have no doubt. The law of mercy can take precedence over the Sabbath law in the case of an ox, so how much more would that be so in the case of a person?

At first sight it looks as though the first six verses of the chapter are unrelated to the following parable. That may be the case but if Luke has taken unrelated incidents and placed them on the same occasion, he has done so for a reason. The Pharisees and experts in the law pride themselves on their correct opinions which put them in right relationship with God and give them the right to places of honour at the table in the great banquet of heaven. They were pushing themselves forward to show that they maintained their own purity by their keeping of the law.

These Pharisees and legal experts were watching Jesus carefully so they could point out how much better they were in God's eyes. They would look down on those less pure, those who were unclean, those who were sick, and make Jesus guilty by association if he related to them. As so often, in this chapter Jesus turns the situation upside down.

This is more than advice about which seats to choose at dinner parties. It is a warning against pushing oneself forward at the event where God is the host. It is a warning against having too high an opinion of yourself and it is also a warning about having too low an opinion of others.

By the time Luke was writing, it is clear that Jesus' message was about more than people's opinions of themselves in relation to others in God's sight. There was then the specific application to Jews and Gentiles at the dinner party of God's Kingdom. Jews – even those who had become Christians – were so used to assuming their place at the top table was deserved because of their descent from Abraham that they couldn't understand that places were granted by God out of grace, mercy and generosity.

Much more than a piece of practical advice for social occasions, this story becomes a salutary lesson for us all in terms of our attitudes to who comes close to God and who doesn't.

The attitude under attack is pride because that is what blocks out God's generous healing love. An attitude of pride says that I deserve God's favour and therefore someone else doesn't. Putting oneself forward to leave others behind is undone by the open-hearted, generous love of God who brings forward the humble, the ones who have been shut out, the least expected, the last to turn up and those who have lost their way. If we have a place at the table already, Jesus teaches us that we have it not because we deserve it but because God's generous open-hearted love has already welcomed us.

If God has already welcomed us, he is just as likely to do the same for the man with dropsy; the woman whose past is at best questionable; those who choose mercy and compassion before strict legal observance; those who have had no opportunity to study; and those who struggle to work, to make relationships, or whose talents, resources or intelligence are less than others'.

We demonstrate our place at the table rather than earn our place at the table when we treat others with the same generous honour as we have already received. When we humble ourselves and treat those with disadvantages with honour and generous hospitality, then we are living with a dependence on God's grace, mercy and love.

16

Jesus on Celebrations

The Wanderer Returns

Luke 15:11-31

Jesus continued: 'There was a man who had two sons. The younger one said to his father, "Father, give me my share of the estate." So he divided his property between them.

'Not long after that, the younger son got together all he had, set off for a distant country and there squandered his wealth in wild living. After he had spent everything, there was a severe famine in that whole country, and he began to be in need. So he went and hired himself out to a citizen of that country, who sent him to his fields to feed pigs. He longed to fill his stomach with the pods that the pigs were eating, but no one gave him anything.

'When he came to his senses, he said, "How many of my father's hired servants have food to spare, and here I am starving to death! I will set out and go back to my father and say to him: Father, I have sinned against heaven and against you. I am no longer worthy to be called your son; make me like one of your hired servants." So he got up and went to his father.

'But while he was still a long way off, his father saw him and was filled with compassion for him; he ran to his son, threw his arms round him and kissed him.

'The son said to him, "Father, I have sinned against heaven and against you. I am no longer worthy to be called your son."

'But the father said to his servants, "Quick! Bring the best robe and put it on him. Put a ring on his finger and sandals on his feet. Bring the fattened calf and kill it. Let's have a feast and celebrate. For this son of mine was dead and is alive again; he was lost and is found." So they began to celebrate.

'Meanwhile, the elder son was in the field. When he came near the house, he heard music and dancing. So he called one of the servants and asked him what was going on. "Your brother has come," he replied, "and your father has killed the fattened calf because he has him back safe and sound."

'The elder brother became angry and refused to go in. So his father went out and pleaded with him. But he answered his father, "Look! All these years I've been slaving for you and never disobeyed your orders. Yet you never gave me even a young goat so I could celebrate with my friends. But when this son of yours who has squandered your property with prostitutes comes home, you kill the fattened calf for him!"

'"My son," the father said, "you are always with me, and everything I have is yours…"'

I always think Jesus must have been really cross at this point. I can think of no other place where he tells three stories one after another to make essentially the same point.

As always, a glance at the context helps.

Now the tax collectors and sinners were all gathering round to hear Jesus. But the Pharisees and the teachers of the law muttered, 'This man welcomes sinners, and eats with them.'[44]

---

[44] Luke 15:1

Jesus then told the story of the lost sheep and the lost coin before he continued from verse eleven with the story we know as the Parable of the Prodigal Son[45]. The main point of the story is clear and is essentially the same as the other two in the chapter. The Pharisees are being snooty about who's in God's good books and who isn't, and Jesus' stories show God's wonderful love, grace and forgiveness in seeking out and welcoming back those who have gone far from him and show any sign of repentance.

The last of the stories is by far the longest, and the cultural references which might be lost on some modern Western audiences give additional insights. All three characters are well drawn in Luke's narrative which is punctuated by references to food.

The first is in relation to the younger son when he is in a distant country. We might assume that his *"wild living"* involved quite a bit of food and drink as well as the prostitutes mentioned later by his older brother. The *"wild living"* is an indirect reference to food, but after he'd spent all he had, the story says everything went wrong for him. He was in need not only because he'd run out of resources but also because there was a famine. Food was scarce and therefore expensive. A desperate situation called for desperate measures.

Just how desperate, we don't realise, until we remember some of the cultural background. It was culturally shameful, and equivalent to wishing his father was dead, to ask for his share of the inheritance. To Jewish ears the story indicates just how far he had gone when we are told that he hired himself out to a citizen of that country and went to feed his pigs. He had sunk as low as it is possible to go when he was hungry enough to be sharing the food of pigs.

There are many classic conversion testimonies that describe a point when someone has hit rock bottom. They've sunk as low as they can go and it is from the depths of despair that they cry out to someone, something – *anything* – and life takes a turn for the better. This may be because God intervenes directly. Or it might be that someone makes an offer of grace and mercy in some form which is (rightly) interpreted as God's way of extending hope and love. Or it might be that the individual sees from the depths of despair that the

---

[45] See Luke 15:11-32

only way is up and from that perspective is able to see a way to turn life around by making a particular decision.

In the case of the younger son in Jesus' story, he *"came to his senses"*. There was no direct intervention; there was no kindly offer from someone to pay his bills or the first month's rent on a flat. From the perspective of rock bottom, he remembered where he had come from. The lack of food and the desire to share the food of pigs reminded him that he used to be a son in a well-off household where he stood to inherit half the estate and where there were servants who were better off than he was in his pit of despair.

Sometimes it is when things are bad that we can see ourselves in proper perspective and *"come to our senses"*, seeing how life could be – perhaps *should* be. This young man not only saw that his father's servants had food when he didn't; at his lowest point he could see that he had done wrong.

In telling the story Jesus says that the young man made up his mind to go back to his father and say, *"Father, I have sinned against heaven and against you. I am no longer worthy to be called your son..."*[46]

For many people their story about coming to God and realising the personal effect of Jesus on their lives involves getting to grips with sin. This part of Jesus' story helps us to see something of what we mean by sin. In this case it is not so much that he has committed an offence under any written code of law. He has made a mess of his relationships in the family with his father and with his brother. His actions have probably had an effect on his father's servants and employees because half the business had been sold.

In acknowledging that he had sinned *"against heaven and against [his father]"* he saw that in actions that broke or at least damaged his relationships at home he had also damaged his relationship with God.

It is worth pausing at that point, before we come to the last references to food in this story, to ask ourselves whether we need to come to our lowest point to see how our actions damage our relationships and that when we fail to love those around us in the

---

[46] Luke 15:18-19

ways that God wants of us, we also damage our relationship with God.

As we have seen, the main point of the story is the father's reaction when the son returns. We'll come to the party in a moment because that is the reference to food. Before that let's remember that the father has been watching for his son, longing for his return and in another cultural reference his reaction to seeing him approach from a long way off is one of unrestrained delight. He runs – something no senior figure would think of doing – and he throws all dignity to the winds.

Of course, the party is the main point. As Jesus put it at the end of the previous two stories, *"there will be more rejoicing in heaven over one sinner who repents than over ninety nine righteous people who do not need to repent"*[47], *"there is rejoicing in the presence of the angels of God over one sinner who repents"*[48].

In this case we get a description of the party and the clothes and jewellery provided for the unexpected guest in whose honour this impromptu party is held. The menu is specifically referred to: *"...bring the fattened calf and kill it."*

So there was a calf fattened ready for a celebration. The father was watching and waiting for his son to return or he wouldn't have seen him coming from such a distance. He had a calf fattened ready for a party. The story is often about the younger son and how we *"come to our senses"*, perhaps at our lowest point, and return to God's ways. But it is also about the father. Usually Jesus' stories are about God, how God relates to us and how God loves us. In this chapter they are about how God longs for us and rejoices to have us among his household. The father who watches and runs and throws a party and has a calf fattened ready for his son's unknown return date shows us a God who longs for us to come to him and throws his arms wide to welcome us and is ready to throw a party like no other at a moment's notice when one who has wandered far from him comes safely home.

But there is a third character. When we read stories, it can be illuminating to our self-awareness to see which character we most

---

[47] Luke 15:7
[48] Luke 15:10

naturally identify with. It can be even more illuminating to ask ourselves, "How would it be if I were a different character?"

In this case, how would it be if you were the elder brother? How does that feel?

The story is brilliantly crafted. The elder brother is clearly the character that Jesus' critics are meant to identify with. They know they're the righteous ones. They know they're among the ninety-nine who do not need to repent. As Jesus tells it, they won't acknowledge any connection with the younger son. The servant tells him, *"Your brother has come home,"* but he speaks to the father saying, *"This son of yours..."*

In his angry response to his father, the elder son also makes reference to food and provides Jesus' response to his critics. He complains that the father never even gave him so much as a kid for a feast with his friends. He expresses a spirit of entitlement: all this celebration is coming out of his share of the inheritance. He should have been given a kid for a feast – but surely it was his to use anyway?

That he has *"never disobeyed any command"* of his father is the phrase that seals the Pharisees' identification with the elder brother. That was their boast; they kept all the Law in every particular; they were therefore entitled to a feast and a celebration and all the goodness of God's Kingdom. Weren't they?

But the father's reaction is where Jesus shows that a spirit of entitlement is not the way of God's Kingdom. A spirit of entitlement puts us first and asserts what we believe we deserve without looking at others. Jesus demonstrates in this story that what God favours more highly is an attitude of gratitude.

When we see that people are coming to God's ways and turning from their *"wild living"*, whatever that may consist of, what is our reaction? Do we have a spirit of entitlement because we have been among God's people for many years and we're not sure about these people who come along later with their new ideas, after lives that leave us rather sceptical about how they're going to behave?

The last verse of the parable is the end of the father's reply to the elder brother and should make us pause and recognise this spirit of entitlement and do all we can to replace it with an attitude of gratitude and generosity. *"...we had to celebrate and be glad, because this brother of yours was dead and is alive; he was lost and is found.*[49]

"*...was dead and is alive...*" To this father, this is more than the remorseful return of a wayward son. This is about new life. This has more than a hint of resurrection about it. And where there is resurrection, celebration is necessary: "*...we had to celebrate...*"[50]

And so too, it is necessary that those who identify with the older brother in this parable should also celebrate when anyone – whatever their previous character, whatever their previous occupation, whatever their previous background – who was lost is found, because it is a sign of resurrection and new life breaking out. That is the only way to combat the spirit of entitlement and replace it with an attitude of gratitude and generosity.

---

[49] Luke 15:32
[50] Emphasis added

17

Jesus on Feeding the Family

The Canaanite Woman

Matthew 15:10-28

Jesus called the crowd to him and said, 'Listen and understand. What goes into someone's mouth does not defile them, but what comes out of their mouth, that is what defiles them.'

Then the disciples came to him and asked, 'Do you know that the Pharisees were offended when they heard this?'

He replied, 'Every plant that my heavenly Father has not planted will be pulled up by the roots. Leave them; they are blind guides. If the blind lead the blind, both will fall into a pit.'

Peter said, 'Explain the parable to us.'

'Are you still so dull?' Jesus asked them. 'Don't you see that whatever enters the mouth goes into the stomach and then out of the body? But the things that come out of a person's mouth come from the heart, and these defile them. For out of the heart come evil thoughts – murder, adultery, sexual immorality, theft, false testimony, slander. These are what

defile a person; but eating with unwashed hands does not defile them.'

Leaving that place, Jesus withdrew to the region of Tyre and Sidon. A Canaanite woman from that vicinity came to him, crying out, 'Lord, Son of David, have mercy on me! My daughter is demon-possessed and suffering terribly.'

Jesus did not answer a word. So his disciples came to him and urged him, 'Send her away, for she keeps crying out after us.'

He answered, 'I was sent only to the lost sheep of Israel.'

The woman came and knelt before him. 'Lord, help me!' she said.

He replied, 'It is not right to take the children's bread and toss it to the dogs.'

'Yes it is, Lord,' she said. 'Even the dogs eat the crumbs that fall from their master's table.'

Then Jesus said to her, 'Woman, you have great faith! Your request is granted.' And her daughter was healed at that moment.

Matthew's account of Jesus' encounter with a woman in the vicinity of Tyre and Sidon on the north eastern coast of Israel-Palestine may well prompt our initial question on reading many passages: "What's that all about, then?"

There are many possible responses to this passage. Is it about someone who persuaded Jesus to change his mind? Is it rather odd in that Jesus seems reluctant to help someone? And then he seems quite rude to her. Apart from calling her *"woman"* (which in the culture and time would not have been rude or derogatory), he practically calls her a dog. Jesus' advice that it is not right to take the children's food and throw it to the dogs is not something most parents feel a need to put up as a reminder on their fridge or the dining room wall.

So, what's that all about, then?

Well, as always, our first tool in interpretation is context. Matthew didn't put in the headings and divisions that we find in our Bibles. They are helpful for finding our way around, but they are not part of the text and can get in the way of our understanding when they divide one part from another. This episode in the vicinity of Tyre and Sidon needs to be read in the context of the section before where Jesus is in controversy about food that is clean or unclean and about ritual washing before meals. The question being posed in those discussions is about what makes someone clean or unclean – what makes us holy, what makes us right before God or otherwise. So let's look at that first (verses 10-20).

My second post in ministry was at an Anglican church with quite a high church tradition. They went in for all the ceremony and processions and incense on special occasions. The person who was Sactristan was quite particular about everything being in the right place at the right time. On one occasion I had put my book down on the Altar so I could read from it while I led the service. It was on the white line cloth between me and the plate and chalice. He told me I was contaminating the Altar and the holy things.

I said I thought it worked the other way and that being on the holy table would make the book holy.

In Jesus' day there were strict ideas about what was holy and what was not and what made something 'unclean'.

Jesus turned some of those ideas upside down by his comments. He has been in controversy with Pharisees about keeping the food laws. These laws had been embellished by the tradition so as to be more precise about their meaning and interpretation. Jesus has pointed out the hypocrisy of a position that uses a tradition that had begun as a way to keep aspects of the law as a way round the law. It's a bit like using a legitimate way to reduce your tax bill as a way to avoid tax altogether while saying the government should provide certain services.

Jesus points out that being clean or unclean is not about what you eat and drink or even how you wash, because what it is really about is how you are in the eyes of God. What you eat and drink might affect your body – you might make yourself ill – but you won't make yourself unholy.

What gives an indication about holiness – about the state of your soul and how you are with God – is what comes out: what you say and what you do that reflect the attitudes that you hold.

That seems pretty clear – it means we don't have to worry about having roast pork or ham sandwiches for lunch. A verse that Mark includes but Matthew leaves out of this section is that Jesus declared all foods clean.[51]

In some ways we could stop there and it makes a straightforward point. It's like one of those *"you've heard it said _____ but I say to you _____"* sayings of Jesus elsewhere. In this case he could have been saying, "You heard that there were certain things you shouldn't eat because they are unclean; but I say to you that they won't make you unclean – it's your thoughts and words and actions that make you 'unclean'".

But as we've noticed before, it is always worth looking at the context. Going straight from verse 20 to verse 21 we can see what Matthew has done. He takes an account of an apparently disconnected incident and places it immediately after the conversation about what is clean and what defiles.

Matthew could have described events that happened as they travelled to the region of Tyre and Sidon. Matthew could have told us something about the conversation they had as they walked. But he didn't – at least not here – because he wanted us to see these two things together.

It seems disconnected.

Jesus left that place and went off to the territory near the cities of Tyre and Sidon. A Canaanite woman who lived in that region came to him. "Son of David!" she cried out. "Have mercy on me, sir! My daughter has a demon and is in a terrible condition."

But by putting the two together it looks as though Matthew is telling us that in this incident Jesus shows us what happens if we 'go by the book' and therefore how faith and holiness and God's relationship with us is meant to work.

If we look at the obvious – the outward appearances and what the Law says about the situation – this is a foreign woman approaching Jesus. We might remember something similar if we think of the incident of the Samaritan woman at the well[52]. In that case John tells us there should have been no communication between them. Here Matthew tells us that Jesus is playing it by the book and he doesn't answer.

---

[51] Mark 7:20
[52] John 4 and chapter 7

It's as though the disciples realise that by her attention and her pestering, she might defile him by leading him into conversation with someone he shouldn't relate to. They try to get him to send her away and Jesus seems to go along with it. He refers to current expectations of the Messiah: he was sent to bring Israel back into line with God; others are not his concern.

So far it is straight down the line, playing by the rules.

Matthew indicates, by the way he tells about her persistence in coming and kneeling at his feet, that she has seen something more in what Jesus is about. Matthew hides more Jewish rules and attitudes in Jesus' reply to her:

"It isn't right to take the children's food and throw it to the dogs."

The children are clearly God's children, the children of Israel – God's holy people.

"Dogs" is not just an extremely offensive way to refer to a woman seeking help; it was also a reference to her 'non-Jewish' status. Jews, offensively, referred to Gentiles as 'dogs'.

Still playing it by the book, Jesus expresses the attitudes that can come out if you see holiness as defined only by what you take in. All of Jesus' words could almost be in quotation marks as though he were saying, "This is what we're meant to say, isn't it? Now, just look what happens if we do that."

He must have been able to see what sort of person she was; he must have known she was persistent and perceptive. She understood about what God was about in his generosity and that if God was going to rule it wouldn't be just over Israel. She seemed to understand that what God gives overflows and that the whole point was always that Israel should show the way for everyone to be God's people, not exclude people because they happened to have the wrong parents.

She picks up the truth of Jesus' illustration, but she points out that it doesn't fully support his point. It *is* wrong to take your children's food and give it to the dogs. Parents don't need reminding of that. But when children drop some of their food, or when your provision has been overgenerous, it is right that the dogs get to eat up the leftovers. God provides enough for his children and others of his household, even the dogs that run around the children's feet.

So Matthew shows us a Caananite woman with a better understanding of what God is about than the Pharisees and teachers of the Law. Because she better understood God and was persistent and perceptive in pursuing what she knew he could and wanted to give, Jesus recognised her faith.

And the scraps fell from the table and she was fed as much as she wanted by the healing of her daughter.

OK, that's not all that happened, but hopefully something of what it's all about. Yet it is still slightly short of satisfactory. This is not just about gaining a better understanding of a piece of the Bible. That might be good and interesting but it's not really good enough if we're to be anything of an outward-looking church as well as a learning church.

This is a kind of "So?" moment.

Let's go back to the simple conclusion from Jesus' explanation of the Law: that it is not what you eat that makes you clean or otherwise but what comes out of you in words and actions and attitudes.

Trying to keep this simple rather than exhaustive, let's ask what actions and attitudes this episode with the Canaanite woman indicate are part of a person who is 'clean', who is holy, who has understood God and can be said to have faith?

One is humility.

That's sometimes a misunderstood word. It is not about being a doormat and just letting everyone else have their way while you get trampled underfoot. Humility is about getting yourself in proper perspective; being realistic about yourself rather than putting yourself across as best or better than others. And it is about being realistic about others and not putting them down in order to put yourself across in a better light.

This woman demonstrated humility almost to the point of self-humiliation. She knew her position: she had a sick daughter and here was someone who could help her, and she was becoming desperate. She will have known she went beyond the rules but she *"fell at his feet"*. She didn't get up close and put her face next to his and demand something; she simply asked for help.

That brings us to another attitude which she demonstrated: boldness in prayer. Sometimes the way things are supposed to be done works against what is clearly the right thing to do. Sometimes human rules made for good reasons (or bad) make it hard to follow God's ways. In such circumstances this woman teaches us it is right to pray boldly for the right thing, the thing that is in accord with God's Kingdom.

There is much in the world that points out and reinforces divisions. As I write, there is a crisis over the Korean peninsula at a time when some have marked the liberation of Korea. It seems ironic that half of the peninsula is clearly not free.

At the same time there are violent disturbances in America over attitudes to the country's history of racial segregation. The same kind of attitudes spill over into the way people treat members of other racial or religious groups, lumping all Muslims together with violent Jihadists.

- God is about unity.
- God is about people coming together.
- God is about welcoming all people around his table.

Maybe we should be praying for the reunification of Korea. That would be boldness in prayer.

God is not about division between Jews and Gentiles, between male and female, between black and white, between north and south or east and west – nor even between 'clean' and 'unclean'.

As part of the invitation to communion I usually use the phrase, "Come not because any goodness of your own gives you a right to come but because you need mercy and help."

So the main attitudes that this Canaanite woman teaches are humility and boldness.

We can also mention others that, as they come out of us, make us 'clean'. Again, this is not exhaustive, but it is a good summary:

- love;
- joy;
- peace;
- patience;
- kindness;
- goodness;
- faithfulness;

- gentleness; and
- self-control.

As Paul says when he gives it as a list of characteristics of a soul that is aligned with the Spirit of God, there is no law against that. The key thing is that we don't let the laws get in the way of being like that.

Love, joy, peace, patience, kindness, goodness, faithfulness, gentleness, self-control, humility and boldness to pray that God's ways would be known around us – that God's Kingdom would come on earth as in heaven.

18

Jesus on Invitations

The Heavenly Wedding Banquet

Matthew 22:1-14

Jesus spoke to them again in parables, saying: 'The kingdom of heaven is like a king who prepared a wedding banquet for his son. He sent his servants to those who had been invited to the banquet to tell them to come, but they refused to come.

'Then he sent some more servants and said, "Tell those who have been invited that I have prepared my dinner: my oxen and fattened cattle have been slaughtered, and everything is ready. Come to the wedding banquet."

'But they paid no attention and went off – one to his field, another to his business. The rest seized his servants, ill-treated them and killed them. The king was enraged. He sent his army and destroyed those murderers and burned their city.

'Then he said to his servants, "The wedding banquet is ready, but those I invited did not deserve to come. So go to the street corners and invite to the banquet anyone you find." So the servants went out into the streets and gathered all the people

they could find, the bad as well as the good, and the wedding hall was filled with guests.

'But when the king came in to see the guests, he noticed a man there who was not wearing wedding clothes. He asked, "How did you get in here without wedding clothes, friend?" The man was speechless.

'Then the king told the attendants, "Tie him hand and foot, and throw him outside, into the darkness, where there will be weeping and gnashing of teeth."

'For many are invited, but few are chosen.'

We're finding out a bit about organising a wedding banquet as we prepare for our daughter's wedding. No doubt we'll find out more as the date gets nearer, but venues are sorted and a number of other key items are in place. Invitations haven't gone out yet but 'Save the Date' cards have so we're fully expecting that when invitations do go, we'll get replies coming back from friends and family to say they'll be coming.

It means I recognise aspects of Jesus' story about the king who invited people to his son's wedding banquet. We imagine those invited were probably family and friends and others of the royal circle of contacts. But in Jesus' story it looks as though they didn't send any 'Save the Date' cards. The invitations only went out when all the arrangements were in place.

When they got their invitations, the guests all had better things or more urgent things to do. They refused to come and when pressed about it, pleaded urgent matters on their farm or other business engagements that they couldn't or wouldn't rearrange.

That much is just about believable. But then there are four parts to the story that stretch our sense of credibility.

Some of the guests *"seized his servants, ill-treated them and killed them"*[53].

That sounds a bit extreme as a way to treat the person who delivers a wedding invitation.

If that was extreme, then the reaction of the king who was inviting them also seems a bit out of proportion:

---

[53] Matthew 22:6

"The king was enraged. He sent his army and destroyed those murderers and burned their city."[54]

As many families do, the king had a reserve guest list, but it is surprising who was on it. He hadn't drawn up a list of other friends or family that were not quite so close that he would invite in the event of some of the original guests not being able to make it.

The reserve list was not so much a list as a random selection of people from the streets around the town. In the way Matthew records it, Jesus leaves it to our imagination to think of who might be found hanging around on street corners at the time a wedding reception is about to begin. All we're told is that there were bad people as well as good.

So we've got a wedding reception full of random people from street corners: the local low-life, the youths who might otherwise have been skateboarding round the local church car park, or – in more biblical terms – prostitutes, 'sinners', day labourers who hadn't found work and so on.

This brings us to the fourth surprise that seems a bit extreme. One of these characters who has been randomly invited turns up without a wedding suit and the king tears into him, has him bound hand and foot and thrown out in the dark where there is wailing and gnashing of teeth.

It sounds as though this king has a tendency to overreact. He's destroyed a city because some people didn't accept his invitation and he's thrown someone out who came at short notice, invited from the local streets but who didn't happen to have been hanging around on a street corner in wedding clothes.

The question is the usual one: "What's that all about, then?"

This is going to be a tricky parable to interpret so we're going to need the first tool of biblical interpretation.

Context.[55]

Specifically, we need to look at two contexts: the biblical context and the cultural context.

---

[54] Matthew 22:7

[55] Congregations where I preach are getting used to the kind of interaction where this is phrased as a question. Usually there's someone who remembers the answer as it comes up quite often.

Before we come to the biblical context it is worth remembering the general context: that this is Jesus telling a story to make a point. We've seen places where the actions of characters in the story seem a bit extreme. It is in this that we are reminded that Jesus was a Jewish rabbi; he told stories to make a point all the time. Like many story-tellers he tended to exaggerate to make his point more effectively. So we're not going to look too hard at the specifics of the destructive and violent reactions. We will notice where they occur and what the point is that's being made. If we take things too literally it leads us to conclusions that are far from what is intended.

So let's start with the biblical context.

Matthew 22 follows on immediately from Matthew 21.[56]

The end of Matthew 21 has two parables: the parable of the tenants in the vineyard and the parable of the two sons sent to work in their father's vineyard.

And before that, significantly, is a section where Jesus' authority was questioned in terms of whether he was really sent from God or not. Jesus' answer to the question of authority was to ask the chief priests' and elders' opinion of the authority of John the Baptist. When they were unable or unwilling to answer about John the Baptist, Jesus said he wouldn't tell them about his own authority. Instead it looks as though he told three stories back to back making the same point about masters sending servants who were treated badly and whose authority was not recognised.

In the two vineyard stories in chapter 21, the people who are approved of are those who end up doing what the vineyard owner wants. One son ends up working in the vineyard even though he had said he wouldn't; the other vineyard is rented to tenants who will provide the requisite produce as rent at the right time when they're asked for it.[57]

---

[56] This seems like stating the obvious but it is a feature we often ignore that the Gospel writers did not put in the chapter divisions or the headings. These help us find our way around the text but they break it up artificially. Congregations where I preach are getting used to hearing this as a question as well. Question: "What comes before Matthew 22?" Answer: "Matthew 21!"

[57] *Jesus on Gardening* chapters 13 and 15

In the parable of the wedding banquet the guests who are approved of in the end are those who come, rather than those who refuse, but they're the ones who not only come but wear their wedding clothes.

That almost brings us to a piece of cultural context that we need in order to interpret this parable. Before we come to that, there's one more piece of biblical context that we need.

It is not an accident that Jesus chose a wedding banquet as the setting for his story. It could have been a birthday party or a retirement party or a bar mitzvah or the celebration of a work anniversary or just a party for the sake of having a party. That would have gone part way to making the point. The setting of a meal is an important symbol for God's welcome and hospitality for his people. But it wasn't any of those other possible settings; it was a wedding banquet.

When we read about a wedding banquet, we're meant to make the connection with the coming of God's Kingdom. A wedding banquet is meant to say, this is about the establishment of God's rule; this is about when God welcomes his people into the place where his ways are followed by everyone; this is where God and his people celebrate their coming together and their being together.

So it will help to have some understanding of the cultural norms around weddings in Jesus' time.

There are various traditions around weddings.

When we got married it was the custom that you had a receiving line – hence 'reception' – as guests arrived at the reception. It seems that doesn't happen anymore. At our daughter's wedding reception, the guests will arrive and be seated and then the Bride and Groom will make their grand entrance.

It is still the case that the principal men will be expected to dress in the same suits, but it is a social disaster for any of the women to be dressed the same except the bridesmaids.

These are traditions. Even around weddings, which we think of as being as traditional as any event, the most noticeable thing about the tradition is that it changes.

So what features of their tradition do we need to have in mind that might explain some of the aspects of Jesus' story that seem a little odd?

The main oddity is this person who has managed to get in without his wedding clothes. Most people will dress up for a wedding but it can be hard to see the difference between wedding clothes and any other fairly smart clothes that might be worn to any party or special occasion. We think that the one without wedding clothes shouldn't have been expected to have them. He was selected at random from a street corner; he was probably in his skateboarding clothes or about to go to the allotment.

There was a custom at the time that guests for a wedding would have been provided with a robe to wear. It may have been given out at the beginning of the receiving line as guests came in to shake the hand of the bride and groom and their parents. It meant everyone would be dressed the same, there would be no competition for who had the most expensive suit or dresses from which designer labels.

Someone who was not wearing the wedding clothes had refused them, or at least avoided those who were giving them out.

OK – now we're in a position to answer our question, "What's that all about, then?"

There's something here about respect.

The guests who refused the invitation in the first place showed no respect for the king who invited them. Their own businesses and their farms were more important, and the way they treated the messengers indicated they wanted nothing more to do with the king who invited them, even though they were presumably in that king's circle of family and friends.

The guest who came under Plan B but didn't put on the wedding robe also showed a lack of respect. His actions make it look as though he thought accepting the invitation was enough and he could be above the need to appear the same as everyone else. He didn't respect the king who provided robes for all his guests, good or bad – he was saying, "Look at me; I don't need to wear a robe."

It's hardly surprising he was speechless when he was taken down more than a peg or two.

Another part of the subject of respect is that it is a word on the same continuum as worship. By pushing the reactions of the king to the extreme, Jesus is asking us to notice what it is that we pay most respect to. What is it that we worship? Do we give our attention and our respect – do we offer worship – to what we have made? To our material things? Our reputation? Aspects of our culture?

Or do we reserve our greatest respect for the one who made us?

And if we want to say the latter, how can we tell; does it show?

This is where the wedding robes come in again in a symbolic way.

The one without the wedding garment was obviously not what the king wanted. Those who were chosen, those who were welcomed into the banquet even though they weren't on the original list – whether they were bad or good – had put on the garment provided; they looked like wedding guests.

This is emphatically not about what you wear to church. It is about accepting an invitation to God's banquet and then looking like a guest at the wedding banquet of the King – the place where his son comes to reign.

In his letter to the Philippians[58], Paul lists some of the ways in which you can tell if someone looks like a guest at the wedding banquet of the king. We could see them as features of the design of the wedding garment:

Are you of one mind with others who work for the gospel – do you make every effort to sort out your differences with one another? Euodia and Syntyche – sometimes known as Odious and So Touchy – seem to have bickered and criticised, and Paul pointed out that they should come to agreement with the help of the community in which they serve and worship.

Another characteristic of the guests at the wedding banquet of the king is continuous rejoicing because we know that God is on the throne, he has the victory in Jesus' resurrection, and we are invited to the wedding banquet.

Then there is gentleness – perhaps unlike characters in Jesus' stories, his followers are to be gentle in their handling of others, not harsh or violent in speech or action. That's one to be aware of among our family, friends and colleagues. It doesn't mean being a doormat or ineffective; it means being firm about what is right but gentle in the way you express it.

---

[58] When this parable comes in the *Revised Common Lectionary,* the New Testament reading is Philippians 4:1-9. Other passages could be chosen to indicate features of the wedding garment, such as Galatians 5:22-23, the fruit of the Spirit.

Another feature of the design of this wedding garment is peace. That's an internal peace that comes whatever is going on around. God's presence to strengthen and to guide in all we do is enough to overcome all difficulty and frustration as we let him know about all that we find overwhelming in our prayers. It is also about an external peace that we work for in any situation.

- Where there is disagreement like that of Euodia and Syntyche, we find ways to bring them to one mind.
- Where there is division in families or communities, we work for reconciliation.
- Where there is division nationally over an issue, we do all we can among our own contacts as well as by joining campaigns and signing petitions to promote a way forward that goes beyond difference, towards consensus.

Finally, Paul gives us a list of characteristics that we are to give reverence to because they build the character of a guest at the wedding banquet of the king:

...whatever is true, whatever is noble, whatever is right, whatever is pure, whatever is lovely, whatever is admirable – if anything is excellent or praiseworthy – think about such things.[59]

These things will be displayed on the wedding garment.
And we might add, as Paul put it to the Colossians:

And over all these virtues put on love, which binds them all together in perfect unity.[60]

That's the best summary of the wedding garment.

- In your relationships do you look as though you're a guest at the wedding banquet of the King?
- At work, at home, at church, in your relationships in other organisations, have you put on love?
- Do you treat people with gentleness when they disagree?

---

[59] Philippians 4:8
[60] Colossians 3:14

- Do you focus on criticism and what is wrong with something or do you focus on what is true, right, pure, admirable, excellent or praiseworthy in order to promote peace and harmony?

The challenge in this story is not so much the interpretation of the rather harsh reactions but to behave as those who are invited to the wedding banquet of the King. The challenge is to demonstrate our worship for the one who invites, and our love for those around us – rather than assume we get in because we move in the right circles.

19

Jesus on Memorable Meals (i)

The Last Supper

Matthew 26:17-30

On the first day of the Festival of Unleavened Bread, the disciples came to Jesus and asked, 'Where do you want us to make preparations for you to eat the Passover?'

He replied, 'Go into the city to a certain man and tell him, "The Teacher says: my appointed time is near. I am going to celebrate the Passover with my disciples at your house."' So the disciples did as Jesus had directed them and prepared the Passover.

When evening came, Jesus was reclining at the table with the Twelve. And while they were eating, he said, 'Truly I tell you, one of you will betray me.'

They were very sad and began to say to him one after the other, 'Surely you don't mean me, Lord?'

Jesus replied, 'The one who has dipped his hand into the bowl with me will betray me. The Son of Man will go just as it is written about him. But woe to that man who betrays the Son of Man! It would be better for him if he had not been born.'

Then Judas, the one who would betray him, said, 'Surely you don't mean me, Rabbi?'

Jesus answered, 'You have said so.'

While they were eating, Jesus took bread, and when he had given thanks, he broke it and gave it to his disciples, saying, 'Take and eat; this is my body.' Then he took a cup, and when he had given thanks, he gave it to them, saying, 'Drink from it, all of you. This is my blood of the covenant, which is poured out for many for the forgiveness of sins. I tell you, I will not drink from this fruit of the vine from now on until that day when I drink it new with you in my Father's kingdom.'

When they had sung a hymn, they went out to the Mount of Olives.

The most memorable meals I've had were all associated with particular occasions. There are lunches and teas to celebrate birthdays and anniversaries and Christmas dinners which spring to mind. What makes them memorable, unlike the lunches, dinners and teas that I have every day, is the occasion they're associated with. We probably did make a special effort with the food but that wasn't what makes it memorable. Christmas dinner isn't just memorable because we have turkey – we do occasionally have turkey on other days and I don't remember those meals.

Passover, for Jesus and his followers, would have been a memorable meal in a similar way to the way Christmas dinner is for us. There was special food; a greater effort was made with that food than would have been when something similar was eaten on other days; the particular combinations of meat and herbs and wine would have been special; but what made it memorable was the occasion.

Jesus is making preparations. He has arranged where he wants this meal to take place and he sends disciples to get everything ready. When the four records of this meal are compared, there are chronological difficulties as to whether it is a Passover meal or comes the day before. There are insufficient details about the meal as a whole to be absolutely clear. It is important not to be obsessive about chronological details or necessarily harmonizing the accounts. Whether the meal was on Tuesday or Thursday, it is in the context of Passover in all four accounts and different aspects are presented in order to make different Passover connections.

Matthew clearly wants us to see the Passover connection with the meal that Jesus is arranging because he points out that Jesus says, *"My appointed time is near."* This is drawn from Mark's account and equates with John's phrase about Jesus' *"hour"*. It refers to Jesus' death, not the meal and not his return. We are meant to see that Jesus' death and Passover are connected and that this meal somehow will tie the two together.

Of course, another aspect of these days that played an essential role in bringing Jesus to his death was his betrayal by Judas. The conversation at this meal about betrayal is something else that makes it memorable. That it was necessary and that Jesus saw it coming don't lessen the nature of it. We have all been cheated from time to time. We may also have perpetrated some form of deceit. But betrayal is very final. It implies the breaking and reversing of friendship. This is not on the level of borrowing a few pounds that you have no intention of repaying. This is more like someone seducing their friend's spouse. Judas has been with them all the way from Galilee; he has heard the parables, he has seen the healings, he has agreed with Peter that Jesus is the Messiah; he has shouted with the crowds and spread his cloak less than a week earlier as Jesus rode into Jerusalem.

Matthew sets this meal in the context of Judas' preparations for betrayal[61] as much as in the context of Jesus' preparations for Passover and his *"appointed time"*. It is not possible to get to the root of what went wrong for Judas. It would no doubt be interesting to speculate on the product of a combination of time travel with psychoanalysis but it is not our principal concern at the moment. Jesus knew that his time was coming and he knew that betrayal was an essential part of that. He initiates the conversation which is another way in which this meal was memorable.

---

[61] Matthew 26:14-16

Maybe there are meals that you remember because of the conversation. Was there an occasion when someone took an opportunity to mention a difficult subject over a meal? Did you ever choose to mention an issue that needed discussion over a meal? Sometimes it makes it easier, sometimes it doesn't. At least when you're eating you can cover a moment when you need to think something through by taking a bite that needs careful chewing.

In this case Jesus had illustrative props to hand. *"One who has dipped his hand into the bowl with me."*[62] It is not meant to single anyone out; it simply says it is a close friend. This is cruel betrayal, not simply cheating or deceit. They didn't immediately know it would be Judas. Presumably, they were all as surprised as each another that it turned out to be him. When Judas asks as all the others have also done, "Surely not I, Rabbi?" Jesus' response doesn't quite spell it out. It is still slightly cryptic and might be interpreted as, "I'm not saying, but you know what's in your own heart and mind."

Matthew has weaved the strands of betrayal and Passover together to create his atmosphere for a meal that will be truly memorable for all those who were there. He doesn't record the rituals of a Passover meal because he assumes that his readers will have known what they were. As readers from a different time and culture, it helps if we remind ourselves that the lamb and the herbs, the bread and the wine were eaten to bring to mind the Exodus of the Israelites from Egypt. It was a memorable meal because of the occasion. This was about God giving freedom to his people.

Lamb was eaten because that was what was eaten in a hurry on the night of the Exodus. Bitter herbs were eaten to remind them of the bitterness of the slavery of their ancestors in Egypt. Unleavened bread was eaten because in Egypt their ancestors hadn't had time to let it rise. There were various cups of wine which were to remind them of the blood of the lambs smeared on the doorposts and lintels that symbolised the 'passing over' of the angel of death so that the Israelites had freedom from death and slavery.

Jesus takes all this memory from his people's past and acknowledges its presence in that room for him and his friends. There was a prescribed script following a ritual laid down for centuries to

---

[62] Matthew 26:23

make the connection with the past. Jesus says and does something that makes the meal memorable again as he departs from the script and connects all that memory to himself, his present situation and his people's situation. There is the strongest possible implication that the longed-for new exodus from exile and oppression was being fulfilled in their own present. Matthew couldn't have been plainer if he had spelt it out. Jesus' *"appointed time"* is the fulfilment of all their hopes for freedom just as the Exodus had been the culmination of the Israelites' hopes for freedom.

Just as the people of Israel in succeeding centuries were associated with their ancestors' deliverance from Egypt by eating Passover, so Jesus' followers participate in what will be accomplished by his death by taking and eating this food.

> *Jesus took bread, and when he had given thanks, he broke it and gave it to his disciples, saying, "Take and eat; this means my body, my very self."*[63]

In a similar way, with a cup of wine he makes the connection with the blood of the lambs at Passover which were sprinkled to mean that the people shared the blessings of the covenant made at Sinai. By sharing wine that Jesus identifies with his blood which will be spilt in death the next day, he inaugurates a new covenant between God and all people: based upon the covenant between God and the people of Israel through the Exodus and the giving of the Law at Sinai, but extended to *"forgiveness of sins"*. As if a nation's freedom from slavery and oppression were not enough, the new covenant will bring freedom from sin and death.

It is hard to imagine the reaction of those twelve friends and followers around that table with Jesus. Clearly this was radically different from the Passover meals they remembered from previous years. It may well have been deeply troubling, extremely shocking and very puzzling. From the perspective of twenty centuries later it helps if we reconnect with the surprise factor rather than simply take for granted that this is what happened.

We look at what happened, we try to understand what happened and to some extent we have learned to live with the knowledge that we will never completely understand what happened. But we do need

---

[63] Matthew 26:26

to wrestle a little more with what it's all about. Christians for twenty centuries have obeyed Jesus' instruction recorded in other places to *"do this in remembrance of [him]"*.[64] What this is still all about, what this is all about now, is more than being reminded of something from the past.

Many nations celebrate an Independence Day when they call to mind events from the past. In our British calendar we keep Bonfire Night on 5 November to remember an event from the past. We keep Armistice Day on 11 November and Remembrance Sunday on the Sunday nearest to it, also to recall events from the past. None of those are simply history lessons. They remind us that we are who we are as a nation and that we have certain institutions in certain forms because of events from the past. Those events shine a light through the intervening years onto our present.

Just as the Israelites celebrated Passover to recall that those events shaped who they are in their own present, so Christians celebrate Holy Communion to recall that the events of that night and the connections made by Jesus at that supper have made us who we are in our own present. In a very strong sense those events are still happening for us and our communities now. The past is not just called to mind; it becomes present for us, for the forgiveness of our sins and for our salvation, our freedom from death, just as it was for theirs.

Maybe it all seems too much, as perhaps it was for those twelve. Peter still seems unable to grasp the necessary connections with Jesus' death. This supper was memorable for so many reasons – perhaps too many for them to cope with at the time. Only later did everything begin to fall into place. The promises about the dawning of the Kingdom seem to pass them by. They can't quite grasp that until after the darkness of that night and the following day. It continues to haunt us too and we find ourselves in the darkness of confusion, and betrayal in the form of denial and hesitation.

It is important to be reminded by this meal that it also works forwards. Whether you call it Holy Communion, Eucharist, Mass or the Lord's Supper, our participation in it is in our present time looking backwards to see the present working of past events. It is

---

[64] 1 Corinthians 11:24-25; Luke 22:19

also looking forwards to the fulfilment of the past and present. As Jesus put it, *"...that day when I drink it new in my Father's Kingdom."[65]*

In the words of Fred Kaan's hymn:

God! As with silent hearts we bring to mind
how hate and war diminish humankind,
we pause – and seek in worship to increase
our knowledge of the things that make for peace.

...

May we, impassioned by your living Word,
remember forward to a world restored.[66]

Remembering forwards always strikes me as an interesting concept. Fred Kaan has applied the idea to Remembrance Sunday where bringing the events of the past into the present helps us also to bring the hoped-for future into the present in terms of a world broken by warfare restored to peace.

Holy Communion does the same in even wider terms. Bringing the past events of the Exodus and Jesus' death and resurrection into the present helps us also to bring the hoped-for future into the present in terms of a world broken by sin and death restored in the new creation of God's Kingdom.

If we can manage even small glimpses of that past, present and future application each time we *"do this in remembrance of [him]"* it makes the Last Supper and each celebration of Holy Communion a truly memorable meal.

---

[65] Matthew 26:29

[66] Reproduced from *Singing the Faith* Electronic Words Edition, number 698. Words: © 1997, Stainer & Bell Ltd, 23 Gruneisen Road, London N3 1DZ <www.stainer.co.uk>

20

Jesus on Memorable Meals (ii)

The Road to Emmaus

Luke 24:13-35

Now that same day two of them were going to a village called Emmaus, about seven miles from Jerusalem. They were talking with each other about everything that had happened. As they talked and discussed these things with each other, Jesus himself came up and walked along with them; but they were kept from recognising him.

He asked them, 'What are you discussing together as you walk along?' They stood still, their faces downcast. One of them, named Cleopas, asked him, 'Are you the only one visiting Jerusalem who does not know the things that have happened there in these days?'

'What things?' he asked.

'About Jesus of Nazareth,' they replied. 'He was a prophet, powerful in word and deed before God and all the people. The chief priests and our rulers handed him over to be sentenced to death, and they crucified him; but we had hoped that he was the one who was going to redeem Israel. And

what is more, it is the third day since all this took place. In addition, some of our women amazed us. They went to the tomb early this morning but didn't find his body. They came and told us that they had seen a vision of angels, who said he was alive. Then some of our companions went to the tomb and found it just as the women had said, but they did not see Jesus.'

He said to them, 'How foolish you are, and how slow to believe all that the prophets have spoken! Did not the Messiah have to suffer these things and then enter his glory?' And beginning with Moses and all the Prophets, he explained to them what was said in all the Scriptures concerning himself.

As they approached the village to which they were going, Jesus continued on as if he were going further. But they urged him strongly, 'Stay with us, for it is nearly evening; the day is almost over.' So he went in to stay with them.

When he was at the table with them, he took bread, gave thanks, broke it and began to give it to them. Then their eyes were opened and they recognised him, and he disappeared from their sight. They asked each other, 'Were not our hearts burning within us while he talked with us on the road and opened the Scriptures to us?'

They got up and returned at once to Jerusalem. There they found the Eleven and those with them, assembled together and saying, 'It is true! The Lord has risen and has appeared to Simon.' Then the two told what had happened on the way, and how Jesus was recognised by them when he broke the bread.

There are often topics of conversation that you can't get away from. Sometimes it's an incident in the international news like a terrorist attack; sometimes it's a major sporting event; sometimes it's a national event like an election or a Royal Wedding. Perhaps less often there's a topic of local interest which might be a local festival or carnival or a matter of some controversy like a planning application for a development on the edge of the village or a 'rationalisation' of bus services. Whatever it is at the time you read this, you know what

I mean. There is no escaping it, the papers are full of it; if anyone talks at all in the bus queue or on the train, that's what they talk about. Sometimes it's something personal that you can't help talking about whomever you're with, especially if it's someone who shares your connection with the subject.

On the evening of the first Easter Day, it was the events over the weekend concerning Jesus of Nazareth. Everyone in Jerusalem was talking about it. News probably hadn't got far out of the city but as people started to disperse after the festival weekend, that's the first thing they would tell their B&B hosts when they arrived at their first stop on the way home.

Cleopas's companion may have been his wife if he is the same as the Clopas whose wife Mary John reports as having been at the cross with three other women. They had been followers of Jesus, they were personally involved in a major news item and they could talk of nothing else but the events of the weekend. They did so with heavy hearts and long faces and a good deal of puzzlement because they had also heard strange rumours of reports from women who had visited Jesus' burial place early that morning.

I don't know if you can imagine yourself back to that time and that place. What might they have been saying to one another? What feelings and what questions would they have been expressing?

It's hard to put ourselves in that time and place because we can't forget that there have been twenty centuries of reflection on the events of that weekend; we can't forget if we've heard the story before; we can't pretend we don't know things that they didn't know.

But it doesn't mean we have all the answers.

They were chewing it over as they walked; to some extent we continue to chew it over as Christians, and others have, for two thousand years. Those two were literally on a journey and those of us following Jesus today are metaphorically on a journey as we discover what it means for us that Jesus died and has risen.

Most of us puzzle over something and we hope to get some answers as we meet together, talk together or perhaps read a book.

Cleopas and his companion seem to come at this topic from at least two directions. There's the high profile major national news event angle. In our terms it would have been the main item on news bulletins from Friday lunchtime onwards. The famous preacher from

Nazareth, the celebrity rabbi from the provinces, had got himself into so much controversy with the authorities, both religious and political, that he'd got himself crucified.

There had been quite a movement that had quickly gathered momentum only a week before. It wasn't just those who pinned their hopes on any popular figure promising freedom and independence. Even some in the Jerusalem bubble were predicting the rise of a new political and religious phenomenon. The question in the papers from Monday to Thursday was whether this could be the national revival everyone had been waiting for.

But controversy during the week and the rising popular movement had caused fear for their position among the establishment. This rabbi was going too far and his promises of freedom that stirred up the masses put what freedoms and privileges they had at risk.

By Thursday evening the mood had swung completely – astute use of social media had put opinion behind a defence of the status quo. By Friday morning they'd got the verdict they wanted and by sundown he was dead and buried.

That was news enough and was still the headlines on the early bulletins on Sunday because on the Sabbath nothing happens. But then came news which gave Cleopas and his companion more to talk about. There came rumours that the tomb was empty and Jesus was alive.

Maybe their conversation went something like this:

Cleopas: Did you hear the news this morning?

Mary: Yes, what did you make of that, then?

Cleopas: I'm not sure – maybe it's fake news.

Mary: Has anyone seen him?

So there was the national level at which it was an inescapable topic of conversation.

But for these two it was also personal. Cleopas and his companion are described as *"two of them"* – the implication is that they were followers of Jesus. They weren't from among the closest of Jesus' friends but they were among those who had followed in some way. If Cleopas's companion was his wife and she was at the cross with Jesus' mother and Mary Magdalene, she must have been one of his closest female followers.

That means that what they discussed was very personal. We get a flavour of it in their response to Jesus' questions. Referring to their personal investment in the national political issue, they said, *"...we had hoped that he was the one who was going to redeem Israel."*

They hoped he was the one who would set the nation free; the one who would rise up in a popular revolt; the one who would revive the greatness of the nation last experienced under King David a thousand years before.

But they also demonstrate that it is personal:

'In addition, some of our women amazed us. They went to the tomb early this morning but didn't find his body. They came and told us that they had seen a vision of angels, who said he was alive. Then some of our companions went to the tomb and found it just as the women had said, but they did not see Jesus.'[67]

Just imagine the thoughts and emotions going through their heads:

- grief and confusion at how matters turned out on Friday;
- fear and anxiety for their own safety;
- confusion and bewilderment at the reports on Sunday morning;
- questions about whether they should be overjoyed but confused because they have never heard of a crucified person being reported to be alive.

Maybe their moods and emotions swung from joy to fear and back to confusion and uncertainty, remembering what was said that morning but not trusting themselves to believe it in case all their hopes were to be dashed yet again.

I never know quite what to make of Jesus' reaction. It sounds a bit harsh given what they've been through:

'How foolish you are, and how slow to believe all that the prophets have spoken!'[68]

---

[67] Luke 24:22-24
[68] Luke 24:25

123

He takes them through the scriptures to show that if they'd read them properly, they should have known it would turn out like this.

I'd love to have been in on that Bible study but the point for us is that they didn't know it was Jesus who was talking them through the prophets from Moses onwards and pointing out how the scriptures showed the kind of saviour they should have expected.

In their hunger for understanding they were fed in an unexpected way by an apparent stranger.

When we stand at bus stops or sit in coffee shops or walk the streets of our neighbourhoods or travel on the train to work, we don't expect to be in the company of someone who will show us how God works among us.

Maybe we should pay more attention to what unexpected people say that encourages us when we're in the depths of despair. Maybe we should listen and watch when unexpected people show kindness and support. No one said it would be easy but the promise is that darkness gives way to light; that despair gives way to hope; that anger, hatred and death cannot hold the powers of mercy, life and love. Maybe we should notice the unexpected ways and the unexpected people who show us those truths.

Hearing something of that message fed them, strengthened them and comforted them. It made sense; they wanted to know more so they invited him in to eat with them when they reached their destination. On the road they were hungry for understanding and had been memorably fed by his words and teaching. Now they must have been physically hungry; they had walked seven miles and it was the end of the day.

The meal served up by their hosts at Emmaus hardly got started. Jesus acted as host when he was the guest. Giving thanks he broke the bread and they recognised him, and as he disappeared their hunger evaporated. That meal was most memorable for not having been eaten.

One of the churches where I minister has a large, light sanctuary at the back of the building and a coffee shop area at the front. There are some parallels in this story with the shape of that building.

We go from the holy place – the Jerusalem – of the sanctuary, to the 'secular' place, the ordinary place of the Coffee Lounge at the front. We go to the place where those of us who have been close to Jesus on a Sunday can talk about what we've seen and heard.

We also go to a place where we meet people we can listen to. In that place we need to be open to hearing a new perspective on Jesus. What we hear might make us see the things of Jesus in a new light. It might help us interpret the things of Jesus in the lives and words of the strangers we meet and talk with.

Both the sanctuary – the holy place – and the Coffee Lounge – the ordinary, everyday place – are places of hospitality. In the sanctuary all are welcome to hear and see something of Jesus in worship and know his presence and hospitality around his table in communion. But in the 'everyday' space there is also hospitality. We call it the Open Door Coffee Lounge because it is a place of welcome for all, a place where all may encounter the words and works of the living Jesus in any and all of those who come – not just the ones who have come from the 'religious' space.

Let's think about that moment of recognition. We usually look at this passage in the context of communion, the holy place where we recognise Jesus' presence in the breaking of bread. But let's remember that they were not in the holy place, they were not in Jerusalem, they were not with the company of believers.

In most church communities this is more like recognising Jesus' presence in the coffee shop over coffee and biscuits than over bread and wine in church.

So we come to their response when they recognised him.

Two of Jesus' followers – those who had been with him and heard from him and knew him reasonably well – recognised him not in the holy place, not where they might have expected to find him, not even in his teaching, but in the stranger who did something wholly unexpected and did something unexpectedly holy.

They recognised him in his hospitality and then they turned to each other and said, 'Oh-h-h! We should have known before!'

The penny dropped – and what did they do?

They got up and returned to Jerusalem.

In half a verse they cover the seven miles it has taken fifteen verses to travel in the outward journey. It gives the impression of them rushing back. When they recognised that Jesus was there on the road and at the inn, in the words and in the hospitality; when they realised that the reports that had caused so much confusion in the early morning had been absolutely right and really they shouldn't have been surprised, they had to go back and share it; they had to go back to be with the others; they went back to the gathering of followers.

In a sense Cleopas and Mary had recognised Jesus among the coffee shop clientele on a Wednesday morning. Their reaction was to make sure they came back to the congregation on Sunday to share what they had seen and heard. So it is two-way traffic. We go from church to share what we have found by being with Jesus in word and worship. But we also go from our coffee shops and offices, schools, factories and leisure centres to share with the community of faith how we have found him in the secular spaces.

Both are absolutely necessary for living the life of a follower of Jesus.

If he'd had it available, Cleopas would have posted it straight onto social media. But even there in that sort of community I suspect he'd have got a similar response. Luke's account reads as though they get back to Jerusalem, gain access to the Upper Room where the other followers have locked themselves in and breathlessly report what happened, and the others hear him and say, "Yeah, we know. Simon's seen him."

Except it's not like that because none of them can contain their joy and excitement:

"It is true! The Lord has risen and has appeared to Simon."[69]

So, whatever the anxiety, whatever the fear, whatever the grief, whatever the heartache, whatever the pain, whatever the questions, whatever the relief, whatever the stress, whatever the tensions – listen for Jesus' words, which are words of comfort and reassurance:

- "No one ever said it would be easy but you have my help and support and guidance."
- "No one ever said it would be a picnic but when you have to drink a bitter cup you have my hospitality – I am there to drink it with you."
- "No one ever said it would be a walk in the park but when you tread the steep and rugged pathway, I am alongside,

---

[69] Luke 24:34

showing the way, holding your hand, carrying you when necessary."

We can say all that because it is true; the Lord has risen and has appeared to Simon and Sheila and Reg and Ann and Margaret and...

21

Jesus on Fish Supper

Resurrection Appearance

Luke 24:36-49

While they were still talking about this, Jesus himself stood among them and said to them, 'Peace be with you.'

They were startled and frightened, thinking they saw a ghost. He said to them, 'Why are you troubled, and why do doubts rise in your minds? Look at my hands and my feet. It is I myself! Touch me and see; a ghost does not have flesh and bones, as you see I have.'

When he had said this, he showed them his hands and feet. And while they still did not believe it because of joy and amazement, he asked them, 'Do you have anything here to eat?' They gave him a piece of broiled fish, and he took it and ate it in their presence.

He said to them, 'This is what I told you while I was still with you: everything must be fulfilled that is written about me in the Law of Moses, the Prophets and the Psalms.'

Then he opened their minds so they could understand the Scriptures. He told them, 'This is what is written: the Messiah

*will suffer and rise from the dead on the third day, and
repentance for the forgiveness of sins will be preached in his
name to all nations, beginning at Jerusalem. You are witnesses
of these things. I am going to send you what my Father has
promised; but stay in the city until you have been clothed with
power from on high.'*

Most of us tend to form a composite picture of Easter from our
knowledge of the Gospels even if we don't quite remember what's in
each one. This passage is Luke's account of the evening of Easter
Day. So a number of those events have already taken place. We might
particularly remember that a number of women discovered that
Jesus' body was missing from the tomb; that Jesus appeared to Mary;
that two disciples were accompanied on their walk to Emmaus by
someone they didn't recognise until they sat down to eat.

This event in the Upper Room in Jerusalem follows on from that
episode.[70] It sounds a lot like another episode we might remember
which is described in John chapter 20:

*On the evening of that first day of the week, when the
disciples were together, with the doors locked for fear of the
Jewish leaders, Jesus came and stood among them and said,
"Peace be with you!" After he said this, he showed them his
hands and side. The disciples were overjoyed when they saw
the Lord.[71]*

It sounds very similar and the differences in the way the account
is related can probably be explained by different writers wanting to
emphasise different aspects.

When you meet someone, I suspect that the main aspects you
notice about them are to do with their appearance. It might be hair
colour, or whether they've combed it. It might be whether they smile
at you or how tall they are or what they're wearing.

Appearance is the first key part of this story. We will look at
some teaching, a commission and a promise as well, but it all rests on
the appearance.

---

[70] Luke 24:13-33
[71] John 20:19-20

The appearance of Jesus is the bulk of the passage. Luke focuses on the physicality of this event. It is clear that Luke wants us to know that this is a real, resurrected Jesus, not a ghost or imagination or even a resuscitated corpse. This is a resurrected Jesus, a healthy, physical, alive Jesus who simply appears among them in spite of locked doors. It is Jesus restored to life but a life that has a qualitative difference to it though many aspects remain the same as the life they know. It is because by his resurrection Jesus has come to inhabit both parts of God's creation: heaven and earth. Only at the end and fulfilment of all things with the new creation will they finally and properly be brought together.

That is why it is so hard to get into the minds of those disciples even though we may be fairly familiar with the whole story. That evening they were still in grief at Jesus' death only just over two days before. They were still in shock at the speed of it all, still in bewilderment at the rumours of him being raised, still puzzled by what that could mean. John's account of that evening points out that they were still in fear. They were afraid of the Jewish authorities because of what had happened to Jesus. They may well have been afraid of the Roman authorities because of the possible implications of him being missing from the tomb.

However much we can see that Jesus had predicted his return and that the Old Testament predicts his return and that it should have been expected, they did not expect it. And even if they had, it was not expected to be like this. If there were any expectations, they would have been much more heavenly, final and apocalyptic, restoring the Kingdom to Israel.

This was not what they expected – this was the Jesus they had known and loved, the man they'd walked with on the dusty roads of Palestine, talked with in the calm of hills above, eaten with by the lakeside and in the houses of dignitaries and friends and in an upper room much like the one they were in now.

They knew this man, knew his face, his voice, his gestures, the look in his eyes...

Except that at the same time it was not the man they knew. This man seemed to appear at will in spite of locked doors. This man seemed to disappear at will from a simple supper just when they were about to start eating.

Luke makes sure to record the ordinary, physical details of appearing suddenly, of hands and feet, flesh and bones. Luke wants to make sure that we know this is not a ghost and he spells it out: *"Ghosts don't have flesh and bones as you can see I have."*[72]

And Luke takes the physical side of it even further. Jesus asked if they had anything there to eat. They must have been having a fish supper and there was a portion left. It's physical, tangible; they watched him eat it. This man was no ghost; this was the man they knew – hands and feet, flesh and blood – eating a fish supper.

It is not what we expect of the returning hero and saviour but it is what we come to expect of Jesus. He is always ordinary in his coming, always understated:

- the maker of the universe born in a manger;
- the sinless one queuing with others for baptism;
- the worker of wonders who heals simply by stretching out a hand or speaking a word of assurance,
- the triumphant king who rides into his city on a donkey;
- the friend who appears out of nowhere but eats a fish supper as though nothing out of the ordinary has occurred...
- and then a few days or weeks later on a beach in Galilee, "Come and have breakfast," as he sits cooking more fish over a charcoal fire.

Luke focuses on the sheer physicality of this man because that's the comfort, that's what makes the difference to their fear and bewilderment and their grief. He's a friend, a teacher – the man they loved. Like a light in the dark, like a fire on a winter evening, like a voice of quiet confidence and reassurance with directions for the disorientated, like a father's embrace, like the clasp of a lover's hand. Perhaps like a fish supper with friends amid great fear and uncertainty.

It is his physical presence that Luke dwells on because it is in his presence that the fear begins to subside

And as the fear subsides, so the joy begins to grow, though it doesn't quite displace the disbelief and the amazement.

---

[72] Luke 24:39

When I take funerals, I am quite often asked to read Canon Henry Scott Holland's piece entitled *Death is Nothing At All*. It is a very comforting piece for those who grieve and in many ways it speaks truth and I point that out for families when I visit them to arrange a service. The one part that is not true is that first phrase, because death is *not* nothing at all. For those who grieve, death is extremely significant; just a few days after any kind of death, perhaps especially one like that of Jesus, death is still high in the minds of family and friends as something final and complete and heart-wrenching that cuts off relationships with so much unsaid, so much unfinished business. The most noticeable thing about life for those who grieve the recent death of a loved one is that their friend, their lover, their partner is not there – there is no escaping the absence.

I read that Fleming Rutledge tells the story of a woman married for many years whose husband died at home. She was calm and efficient with the emergency services, quite composed as efforts to revive him were abandoned. But as his body was taken from the house, she lost it and, sobbing uncontrollably, would not be separated from the stretcher. A nurse tried to comfort her: "It's only his body – his soul has gone to heaven." At this she wept even more, "It's his body that I want!"

Luke spends time on the appearance because it is in his physical presence that they find the comfort; it is his physical presence that helps them to know he has been raised; it is his physical presence that helps them adjust their expectations and move from death to life, to see that death is not the end, that maybe Henry Scott Holland might be a little bit right that death is not such a big thing as they – as we – think and feel.

But his appearance and the comfort of his physical presence is not an end in itself. Luke dwells on it but this report of Jesus' physical presence is not his final purpose. This was all in order to help them understand. And Luke tells it the way he does in order to help his readers understand too. It is only through this understanding that we really get beyond the impact of death.

After he'd eaten his fish supper to demonstrate in a very physical way that he is not a ghost, *"He said to them, 'This is what I told you while I was still with you: everything must be fulfilled that is written about me in the Law of Moses, the Prophets and the Psalms.' Then he opened their minds so they could understand the Scriptures. He told them, 'This is what is written: The Messiah will suffer and rise from the dead on the third day, and repentance for the forgiveness of sins will be preached in his name to all nations, beginning at Jerusalem.'*[73]

This is the second Bible Study on the way the Law and the Prophets are fulfilled in Jesus in one chapter. Cleopas and his companion would know this pretty well by the time they'd finished their fish supper that night.

Jesus demonstrates the continuity: how the Jewish scriptures point to his life, ministry, death and resurrection. Jesus shows how a suffering, crucified and risen Messiah is not a novel idea but a proper understanding and interpretation of the old expectations.

So the appearance makes possible the teaching and that in turn leads to the commission. It's only six words in comparison with all the verses given to the appearance, but so significant: *"You are witnesses of these things."*

Before we return to the commission, we need to notice the promise: Jesus went on, *"I am going to send you what my Father has promised; but stay in the city until you have been clothed with power from on high."*[74]

Neither the comfort of the physical appearance nor the teaching are complete or make sense without the promise. And the commission cannot be contemplated without the promise.

Death is not nothing at all; it is terrible and all our losses are hard to bear. But the resurrection gives us comfort, gives us hope, gives us the possibility of the eternal perspective.

We will grieve but not as those without hope.[75]

We will see our loved ones again; we can live life on a different plane and as we give, laugh, love and celebrate – as we eat and drink, embrace, call out, whisper and reach out and touch, so we are united with Christ in his resurrection and we discover that he has breathed into us the power to be witnesses of these things.

---

[73] Luke 24:45-47, emphasis added
[74] Luke 24:49
[75] 1 Thessalonians 4:13

133

22

Jesus on Breakfast

Breakfast on the Beach

John 21:1-25

Jesus appeared again to his disciples, by the Sea of Galilee. It happened this way: Simon Peter, Thomas (also known as Didymus), Nathanael from Cana in Galilee, the sons of Zebedee, and two other disciples were together. 'I'm going out to fish,' Simon Peter told them, and they said, 'We'll go with you.' So they went out and got into the boat, but that night they caught nothing.

Early in the morning, Jesus stood on the shore, but the disciples did not realise that it was Jesus. He called out to them, 'Friends, haven't you any fish?'

'No,' they answered.

He said, 'Throw your net on the right side of the boat and you will find some.' When they did, they were unable to haul the net in because of the large number of fish.

Then the disciple whom Jesus loved said to Peter, 'It is the Lord!' As soon as Simon Peter heard him say, 'It is the Lord,' he wrapped his outer garment round him (for he had taken it off) and jumped into the water. The other disciples followed in the boat, towing the net full of fish, for they were not far from shore, about a hundred metres. When they landed, they saw a fire of burning coals there with fish on it, and some bread.

Jesus said to them, 'Bring some of the fish you have just caught.' So Simon Peter climbed back into the boat and dragged the net ashore. It was full of large fish, 153, but even with so many the net was not torn. Jesus said to them, 'Come and have breakfast.' None of the disciples dared ask him, 'Who are you?' They knew it was the Lord. Jesus came, took the bread and gave it to them, and did the same with the fish. This was now the third time Jesus appeared to his disciples after he was raised from the dead.

When they had finished eating, Jesus said to Simon Peter, 'Simon son of John, do you love me more than these?'

'Yes, Lord,' he said, 'you know that I love you.' Jesus said, 'Feed my lambs.'

Again Jesus said, 'Simon son of John, do you love me?'

He answered, 'Yes, Lord, you know that I love you.'

Jesus said, 'Take care of my sheep.'

The third time he said to him, 'Simon son of John, do you love me?'

Peter was hurt because Jesus asked him the third time, 'Do you love me?' He said, 'Lord, you know all things; you know that I love you.'

Jesus said, 'Feed my sheep. Very truly I tell you, when you were younger you dressed yourself and went where you wanted; but when you are old you will stretch out your hands, and someone else will dress you and lead you where you do not want to go.' Jesus said this to indicate the kind of death by which Peter would glorify God. Then he said to him, 'Follow me!'

Peter turned and saw that the disciple whom Jesus loved was following them. (This was the one who had leaned back against Jesus at the supper and had said, 'Lord, who is going to betray you?') When Peter saw him, he asked, 'Lord, what about him?'

Jesus answered, 'If I want him to remain alive until I return, what is that to you? You must follow me.' Because of this, the rumour spread among the believers that this disciple would not die. But Jesus did not say that he would not die; he only said, 'If I want him to remain alive until I return, what is that to you?' This is the disciple who testifies to these things and who wrote them down. We know that his testimony is true.

Jesus did many other things as well. If every one of them were written down, I suppose that even the whole world would not have room for the books that would be written.

I often start with questions that create an easy and relevant but slightly sideways angle on the subject to be addressed. In this instance I haven't started with an easy one. The question is, "What is love?"

The responses from congregations and probably from readers who pause at this point to work out their own answers usually cover the following subjects amongst others:

- Affection
- Friendship
- Commitment
- Kinship
- Passion

- Altruism
- Emotional intimacy
- Physical intimacy
- Attachment
- Service

It wasn't meant to be easy and the reason it was hard is bound up in this definition: Love is... *an abstract concept that is easier to experience than to explain.*

I once found a diagram of the brain that attempted to explain what goes on in the brain when someone experiences emotions associated with love. It didn't explain what sort of love was being experienced and looked very complicated. That's probably why love is often symbolized rather than explained. So the easy question is to name the most common symbol for love.

The picture in your mind is probably what most congregations are chorusing: a heart – usually a red one. At this point think valentine cards, for instance. Of course, as a reader of a book with Jesus in the title or a member of a church congregation you may be ahead of me in thinking of the Bible's definition of love from 1 Corinthians 13.

> *Love is patient; love is kind. It does not envy, it does not boast, it is not proud. It is not rude, it is not self-seeking, it is not easily angered, and it keeps no record of wrongs. Love does not delight in evil but rejoices with the truth. It always protects, it always trusts; it always hopes, it always perseveres.*[76]

Of course, that was originally written in Greek and there is much in it that is what love is *not* rather than a positive definition. The most obvious thing to say so far in this exploration of love is that it is hard to define in English because in English we use the same word for a great many different ideas, emotions, actions and attitudes.

When John wrote his Gospel, he wrote in Greek like St Paul who wrote 1 Corinthians. That meant he had more words at his disposal and could differentiate between their meanings.

Much has been made of the fact that he uses two different words for love in the conversation that he records between Jesus and Peter after they finished their breakfast of fish on that beach in Galilee some days or weeks after Jesus' death and resurrection.

If you look through the text of that conversation in an English translation, the question is whether you can tell what meaning for love is used in each case. The right answer is, "No, you can't."

So here's a quick Greek lesson which won't help you much on holiday but if you form a romantic attachment to someone or experience strong physical attraction while you're in Greece, here are two words that are not the ones you want.

Three times Jesus asks Peter, *"Do you love me?"* and three times Peter replies, *"You know that I love you."* But there are two different words that are both translated *"love"* in that passage.

Agapao is the word that Jesus uses in his first two questions.

Peter replies each time using a different word – the word *Phileo*.

---

[76] 1 Corinthians 13:5-7

137

The final third time Jesus asks, *"Do you love me,"* he uses Peter's *phileo* word.

Agapao (Jesus' word) is a voluntary love, a love that you choose, a love that seeks the good of the one who is loved even to the point of self-sacrifice.

Phileo (Peter's word) is an emotional love based on personal, often familial affection.

So, the argument goes that Jesus was asking Peter about the depth of his commitment. "Do you love me more than these? Have you chosen me and committed yourself to me more than these?"

But Peter replied expressing his affection. "You know I'm your friend, you know I'm fond of you, you know I think you're wonderful."

We'll come back to the *"more than these"* part of Jesus' question shortly. Before that it is worth noting the difference in those words. When people are asked which of the disciples they most identify with, many of them put Peter at or near the top of the list. So whether or not you ever identify with Peter, listen to Jesus ask you the same question.

David, do you love me more than these?

Amy, do you love me more than these?

Ben, do you love me?

Emily, do you love me?

[Your name], do you love me?

Do you love me? Do you?

Jesus asks you:

- How committed are you?
- Would you give yourself completely for me?
- *Would* you?

Churches all over the country and indeed all over the world sing, pray and worship, and know a lot about who Jesus was and what he said and what he did. We can fairly easily reach a certain point where we can say, "Lord, you know that I'm fond of you, you know I think you're wonderful, you know I marvel at all you do and all you've done, you know that I love you."

But through this conversation after breakfast Jesus replies, "Actually, that's not what I asked. Do you love me?"

The third time Jesus asks his question he changes his word and uses Peter's *phileo* word so it's a slightly different question. "Are you sure that affection is real and sincere?"

To which it seems Peter replies in a way that we might echo, "Yes, of course it is, I keep telling you. I'm actually quite upset that you don't seem to believe me and have to keep asking."

But deep down we know we've been challenged.

Jesus knows that we have a deep personal affection and attachment to him. We think he's wonderful and we want to be with him all the time and know that he's with us – but we also know that he's asked us something rather different and we haven't given a proper response.

So, here's the challenge; here's the centre of this message from this breakfast conversation:

- Have you chosen?
- Is your love for Jesus one that you have chosen?
- Have you made a decision that Jesus is the one whom you can give yourself for?

To put it in the terms used in the conversation between Jesus and Peter, have you moved from affection to self-giving? Have you moved from *phileo* to *agapeo*?

Having reached that central question, it's time to explore two other aspects of Jesus' question.

Jesus starts his first question saying, *"Simon son of John…"*

We thought Jesus was talking to Peter but he calls him *"Simon son of John"*. This is a deliberate device to take Peter back to the first time they met, the first time he called him by the same lake after a similar miraculous catch of fish.[77] It was later that he was given the name Peter and it would be later still that he proved himself worthy of being called 'The Rock'.

"Simon son of John "[78] is a reminder of the past and a reminder of how far they've come together as a group and a reminder of how far Peter has come personally in that time.

The challenge is the same: "Simon, Son of John – yes that Simon, the one who's been with me all this time, the one who came

---

[77] Luke 5:1-11; see chapter 3
[78] Emphasis added

unhesitatingly after that first catch of fish, *that* Simon Son of John, do you love me? Have you chosen?"

We can ask ourselves in the same way, reminding ourselves of the first time we responded to Jesus' call and checking how far our discipleship, our desire to be with Jesus, our discipleship and our love for him has developed.

Then there's the last part of Jesus' question, *"Simon son of John, do you love me more than these?"*[79]

There are three ways to understand this.

1. "Do you love me more than these men love me?"
2. "Do you love me more than you love these men?"
3. "Do you love me more than you love these things?" meaning the fishing gear that would have been lying around after their night's fishing and the catch they'd just had that morning.

So, Jesus asks:

3. Do you love me more than you love the tools of your trade?
2. Do you love me more than you love your friends and colleagues?
1. Do you love me more than these other people love me?

One of the delightful aspects of the Bible's ambiguity in some matters of intent and interpretation is that it leaves space for us to imagine. Here we can pick and choose according to how we imagine the scene and Jesus' tone of voice.

*   How does it sound if Jesus asks you whether you love him more than the tools of your trade?
*   How does it sound if Jesus asks you whether you love him more than you love your family, friends and colleagues?

There is challenge to be had by those interpretations, but the traditional way of understanding Jesus' question is probably the most likely: "Do you love me more than these other people love me?"

The reason that's most likely is that Peter had said he would never desert Jesus; he said he would die with him if necessary; he said he would give himself, even if all the others did desert him. But Peter did desert him and denied that he knew him – three times.

---

[79] Emphasis added

So Jesus asks him, "*Do* you love me, *have* you chosen me as one whom you would give yourself for? *Are* you willing to go further for me than these others? *Do* you love me *more than* these?"

That doesn't mean we need to go comparing our love for Jesus with that of the people around us – unless, of course, we have claimed that our love is greater than theirs. What this does show is that Jesus has an uncanny knack of remembering what we've said and the claims and the commitments we've made. And in this question, it comes back to haunt us – was that true, did you mean that?

- "Do you love me more than these?"
- "Have you moved from affection to self-giving, from *phileo* to *agapeo*, any more than the next person?"

This exchange between Peter and Jesus is wonderful and instructive for so many reasons. We've seen the element of challenge that it had for Peter and also for us in the way the questions and the answers were framed. But each time, Jesus responds to Peter's answer and this sounds a highly encouraging note to the exchange as well.

Jesus: Do you love me more than these?
Peter: You know that I love you.
Jesus: Feed my lambs.
           Take care of my sheep.
           Feed my sheep.

Peter had denied Jesus three times, so Jesus asked him three times, do you love me? Three times Peter had the opportunity to reply and affirm his love for Jesus, and Jesus doesn't rebuke him for using the *phileo* word rather than the *agapeo* word. Rather than rebuke him, Jesus affirms and encourages Peter.

"Because you're fond of me, because you have an affection for me, because you count me your friend and count yourself among my friends, that is enough. You're in, you belong, I have a role for you." If you're in listening mode now, take a moment to hear that.

- Feed my lambs.
- Take care of my sheep.
- Feed my sheep.

The Shepherds of Israel were an important religious, royal and symbolic motif even if the actual shepherds were not wealthy or highly thought of but often on the edges of society. Jesus is saying to Peter, "Be a leader among my people, be the shepherd of the flock, follow in the footsteps of the Good Shepherd."

That is encouraging.

If we have reached the point of being able to say Jesus is someone we want to follow, be with and get to know, he has a role for us. Even if we can't say with confidence that we would go with him to prison and to death, he still affirms us and calls us to be significant among his people.

So, whoever you are, however recently you may have let Jesus down, however unworthy you think you are, hear this from Jesus: he wants you among his closest friends.

That's quite a lot to take in after breakfast following an unsuccessful night's fishing but it does give us both challenge and encouragement. There is also some reassurance from the last part of the conversation.

Peter notices John also on the beach and asks, *"…what about him?"* And Jesus basically says, "What's that to you? You don't have to worry about him. If I take care of you, I'll take care of him."

That's reassuring. We don't have to worry too much about the state of other Christians' relationships with Jesus; we don't have to know what plans or commissions he has for them.

But the challenge comes back at the end. Jesus is saying it all the time. It was the first thing he said to Peter and now it's the last thing he says. He said it to many people during his ministry and he still says it today, and he says it to me and he says it to you.

However you respond to the "Do you love me?" question, still he says, "Follow me."

He said it to fishermen by the lake, he said it to a man who wanted to go and bury his father, he said it to tax collectors, he said it in the context of having no possessions and in the context of his death, he said it to rich people and poor people, and he's gone on saying it to countless millions of people since for 2,000 years – and he's said it to me and he says it to you. "Follow me."

So how do you respond?

That first time, they left their nets and the hired men in the boat and followed him.

Peter said, "I will follow you to prison and to death," and the same night he denied three times that he even knew him. But later – many years after this encounter – he would do exactly as Jesus predicted.

Jesus says, "Whatever I have in mind for Bob or Joan or this person or that person, what is that to you? *You* must follow me."

Let those two short sentences of Jesus echo through your mind:

"Do you love me?"
"Follow me."

Also by David Muskett

Jesus on Gardening
ISBN 978-1-911086-28-4

When Jesus taught, he often used stories that his listeners would be able to relate to – each one revealing something about God's activity on Earth.

David Muskett looks at what Jesus said about horticulture and agriculture – and finds parallels in our British love for gardening.

These short, easily digestible sermons will leave you inspired and empowered to see God's Kingdom grow in your own local neighbourhood.

"…down-to-earth, true to Scripture and gently inspirational…"
Revd David Sutcliffe, Pastor, Hearsall Baptist Church, Coventry

"…written and developed so that we have a better understanding of the call of Christ in our own lives and as we face the challenge of discipleship and faith today."
The Rev'd Andrew de Ville, Superintendent Minister,
The Methodist Church

"…clever and creative…"
Keith Field, Cranleigh Baptist Church

www.onwardsandupwards.org/jesus-on-gardening